MR. LINCOLN'S PROCLAMATION

MR. LINCOLN'S PROCLAMATION

THE STORY OF THE EMANCIPATION PROCLAMATION

By Frank Donovan

ILLUSTRATED

DODD, MEAD & COMPANY

NEW YORK

Fourth Printing

Printed in the United States of America
by The Cornwall Press, Inc., Cornwall, N.Y.

The quotation on pages 48-49 from *Abraham Lincoln: The War Years* by Carl Sandburg is reproduced by permission of the publisher, Harcourt, Brace & World, Inc.

The quotation on page 32 from *The Phantom Public* by Walter Lippmann, Copyright © 1925, renewed 1953 by Walter Lippmann, is reproduced by permission of the publisher, The Macmillan Company, New York.

An Explanation

First, let it be clearly understood that this is not a "debunking" book. Its purpose is not to downgrade the Great Emancipator nor to minimize the long-range importance of his Proclamation. However, it is impossible to tell the story of the Emancipation Proclamation and the events leading up to it without correcting some widely held misconceptions about the purpose and immediate effect of the document. It would be an exaggeration, but only a mild one, to say that the Emancipation Proclamation did not, when it was issued, free *any* slaves.

Lincoln's historic document did not apply to all slaves. Those in the border slave states of Maryland, Delaware, Kentucky, Tennessee and Missouri were not covered by it. Also, slaves in certain parts of Confederate states which were already occupied by Union forces were not emancipated by the Proclamation.

In the areas where it did apply it could not be enforced.

No slaveholder who was in rebellion against the government headed by Mr. Lincoln released his slaves from bondage because the "enemy's" Chief Executive so ordained. In practice, no slave was freed until the military forces of the Union reached his plantation and compelled his release. And the Union Army had been freeing slaves, under an act of Congress, before the Emancipation Proclamation was issued.

At the time that he wrote it, Mr. Lincoln's Proclamation was primarily a military move. Its secondary purpose was political, both at home and abroad. Although Lincoln personally considered slavery immoral and inhuman, these were not the considerations which motivated his document.

In the longer view the Proclamation became a great moral force. And, regardless of its purpose and effect at the time it was issued, it was the decisive step which led to the ultimate extinction of human bondage in the United States. For this reason—and not because, of itself, it freed the slaves—it ranks only below the Declaration of Independence as a milestone on the road to freedom.

Contents

Illustrations

All illustrations are from the Collections of the Library of
    Congress, with the exception of the Preliminary Emanci-
    pation Proclamation in Lincoln's hand, the original of
    which is in the New York State Library.

Illustrations

MR. LINCOLN'S PROCLAMATION

1

Human Bondage

In August, 1619, widower John Rolfe, who still grieved for his dead wife, the Princess Pocahontas, made a casual note in his diary. It said that a ship had arrived off the harbor of Jamestown, "a dutch man of warre that sold us twenty Negars." Other evidence indicates that Rolfe was not entirely accurate. The vessel was a Dutch-commissioned privateer and probably a pirate rather than a man-of-war; and the Negroes were not actually sold. The ship was destitute of provisions, and although the colonists would not permit it to berth, they gave the crew supplies. In return, the privateer left the twenty Negroes, whom they seem to have captured from a Spanish vessel.

The details are not important, but Rolfe's record is. It is the first reference to the most prolonged problem that America has ever faced—the relationship between the white man and the black man.

The status of the early Negroes in the colonies is vague

1

and complicated. As time went on, the status of the Negro became less vague—and much more complicated. It is impossible to draw a cameo-sharp picture of the institution of slavery in America. Few of the long-dead writers and speakers who commented on it were objective. They were either pro or con—or uninformed. As time advanced into the nineteenth century, bitterness and fanaticism begat violent accusations and exaggerations from which it is sometimes impossible to sift indisputable fact. And the record is rife with many ironies. Those who smugly trace their ancestry to the *Mayflower* might remember that the Negroes landed in Jamestown a year before that little ship arrived at Plymouth Rock.

The early colonists accepted human bondage as an unquestioned fact of life. Slavery existed in all societies before written history. The Egyptians enslaved the Israelites; the Israelites enslaved the Canaanites; Babylonians re-enslaved the Israelites. The Romans enslaved the peoples of much of the known world. The Moslems enslaved Christians. The Vikings enslaved anybody they could lay their hands on who might bring a sufficient price to warrant carrying him to market. And so it went throughout history.

Ignoring the Roman conquests, and a Viking raid to the Mediterranean in the tenth century which, according to the ancient Irish annals, brought some "blue men" back to Dublin, the African slave trade of the Middle Ages was started by Prince Henry of Portugal in 1444. Negro slaves were taken first to Europe and later to Spanish America. Spain soon joined the traffic. Columbus mentioned Negroes in the records of his voyages, and thirty Negroes helped Balboa, in 1513, carry some knocked-down ships across the isthmus from the Atlantic to the Pacific at a point very near the site of the Panama Canal.

England joined the unholy business in 1562 when Captain John Hawkins brought back a cargo of blacks from the Guinea coast in a ship named—again, irony—the *Jesus*. One account has the first Queen Elizabeth condemning the nefarious trade, but she later had a change of heart. Perhaps profits, to which the Virgin Queen was addicted, salved her conscience and led her to knight Sir John Hawkins and give him a crest displaying the bust of a Negro with the arms securely bound.

By the time the English colonies were established in North America, Negro slaves were common in the Spanish colonies. They had replaced many Indian slaves whom the Spaniards had worked to death. And bondage of another sort was soon prevalent in the English colonies. In the seventeenth and early eighteenth centuries the life of the "common man" in Europe was so desolate that any change from his hopeless state seemed desirable. He could not hope to acquire the price of a passage to the colonies, but there were many obliging sea captains who would carry him—or her—for nothing. Prospective immigrants merely made their marks on indentures under which they would serve any master to whom they were sold for five to seven years. The sea captain sold these indentures at port of entry for a handsome profit to an agent, and this "soul driver" took the batches of immigrants to the readiest market and sold them as servants or laborers. To those who willingly submitted to bondage were added many likely lads and comely wenches who were kidnapped from London's streets.

England swelled the flood of indentured souls by sending to the colonies criminals who were too petty to hang.

Romantic fiction often presents these transportees as handsome young gentlemen or beautiful young ladies who were victims of circumstances; but, in fact, most of them were the scum of the slums—thieves, pimps, pickpockets and prostitutes. An exception to this were a few political prisoners who were transported; specifically some of those who followed the Duke of Monmouth in his revolt against James II. The system of transporting criminals so irked Benjamin Franklin that he wrote the first of his famous "hoaxes" on the subject, in which he made the tongue-in-cheek proposal that the colonies, in exchange for the criminals, send native rattlesnakes to England where their venomous habits might be refined by the cultured climate of the homeland.

Like all new lands the colonies were hungry for labor, but the more rural South was hungrier than the increasingly urban North. New England could be choosier about immigrants than her southern neighbors. Consequently most of the outcasts who were transported—perhaps fifty thousand during the eighteenth century—were landed south of Baltimore. This would have a later bearing on the status of the Negro. The descendants of many of the transportees became the "poor whites" of the South who, although they were not slaveowners, developed a bitter hatred for the Negro—the only human life to whom they could feel superior. The Negroes, in turn, particularly artisans or house servants, were contemptuous of the "white trash" to whom *they* felt superior.

There was little difference between the condition of the indentured servant and the slave. At the will of his master either could be whipped, starved, mutilated or confined, and the females could be bedded. If the bondsman ran away the law would pursue him, brand him or crop his

ears, and return him to his master. But there was one difference that made *all* the difference. Indentured bondage
was for a limited period. Slavery was for life. And the offspring of indentured servants were born free. Those of
slaves were born slaves.

In the earliest colonial days the Negro was considered
as a bond servant rather than a slave. There were no special
laws covering Negroes, and it was inferred that they might
sometime be freed. The catch was "sometime." The indentured white man was held in bondage for a specific
period of time. With the Negro it soon developed that
sometime never came. Ironically Massachusetts, which
would become the hotbed of abolitionism, was the first
colony to pass a law sanctioning slavery. In 1641 the colony
decreed that "there shall never be any bond slavery, vil-
leinage, nor captivity among us, unless it be lawful cap-
tives taken in just wars, and such strangers who willingly
sell themselves or are sold to us, and these shall have all
the liberties and Christian usages which the law of God
established in Israel requires." The first class of persons
to whom the act referred were Indians. The second, who
"sell themselves," were indentured servants. The third,
who "are sold," were Negro slaves.

Throughout the rest of the seventeenth century and into
the early eighteenth the other colonies passed laws that
either legalized slavery or acknowledged it. Some were
vague, like New York's, which forbade any Christian to be
kept in slavery "except who shall be judged thereunto by
authority." Maryland, in 1663, was the first colony to adopt
a forthright, clear-cut statute on slavery, which provided
that, "all Negroes and other slaves to be hereafter imported
into this province shall serve during life; and all children

born to any Negro or other slave shall be slaves as their fathers were, for the term of their lives."

With or without specific legal sanction, Negro slavery was an established institution by the beginning of the eighteenth century, and was thriving in the southern colonies. In 1720 there were 12,000 Negroes in South Carolina and only 9,000 whites. The Negro was better adjusted to the climate of the South and more suited than white labor to the mass agricultural operations involved in raising rice, indigo and tobacco. The slaves were more stable than indentured white laborers, who had the distressing habit of taking off for the nearby mountains and losing themselves among the pioneer settlers. The Negro's color prevented this. And the slave, once purchased, worked for life. As Benjamin Franklin said, "Why will Americans buy slaves? Because slaves may be kept as long as man pleases or has occasion for their labor; while hired men are continually leaving their masters (often in the midst of his business) and setting up for themselves."

For the first three quarters of the eighteenth century there was little change in the institution of slavery or the attitude toward it. When Jefferson wrote, "all men are created equal" in the document that was a clarion call to freedom, Negro slavery was legal and in effect in all of the thirteen colonies.

Laws governing slavery became more specific. An amusing situation developed in Maryland—amusing, that is, if one were not involved. There was considerable intermarriage—or crossbreeding without marriage—between white indentured servants and Negro slaves. Disturbed at a growing crop of mulatto children Maryland passed a law that a white female servant who bore a child by a Negro slave must serve her master until the death of her husband, and the child would be a slave for life. This offered a fine opportunity to an unscrupulous, avaricious slaveowner to get three slaves for the price of one by forcing his white female indentured servant to breed with his Negro slave. The colony then did a right-about-face and ruled that the mother and child in such a situation would be immediately freed and the master heavily fined.

A rash of laws restricting the few rights of the Negro were passed as a result of a panic in New York in 1741. There were nine fires in the metropolis of 9,000 in rapid succession. Through the initial testimony of a half-wit girl and a white prostitute several Negroes were implicated. The case developed into a mad, unreasoned witch hunt which ended with fourteen Negroes being burned at the stake and eighteen hanged. There was no solid evidence that the Negroes were in any way involved in the fires.

The fear of a Negro insurrection swept the South—and remained ever present throughout the slavery era. Realizing that revolt required organization, that organization required leadership, and that leadership usually involved a developed mind, the South passed laws which prohibited Negroes from learning to read.

It was also illegal, in some places, to give a Negro religious instruction. Many of the early descendants of the pious Christians who had come to the New World to gain religious freedom denied their faith to the Negro. This was based on the warped concept that a heathen Negro would be benefited by being a slave to the white man, but the Christian conscience rebelled at the enslavement of another Christian. The solution to this moral dilemma was simple—deny the boon of faith to the Negro and keep him as a slave with a clear conscience. In North Carolina a free Negro who gave a slave a Bible—or any other book—was

punished with thirty-nine lashes. A white man was fined
$200.

In the final years of the century the laws governing
Negroes became so strict that they lost the last semblance
of human rights. This sprang from the successful slave
revolution in Haiti in 1787, which established the island
as a black empire. Quaking white refugees from Haiti told
nightmare tales of slaughter and rapine by the blacks, of
burning mansion houses, masters tortured and beheaded
while their wives and daughters were raped. The white
South shuddered in fear and passed laws to so suppress the
Negroes that revolt would be impossible.

These laws bore as heavily on free Negroes as on slaves.
There were a few such—about 8 per cent of the Negro
population in the first census taken in 1790. Some had
gained their freedom by rendering an outstanding service
to the community. Some had been freed by kindly masters
in their wills, although in several states voluntary manu-
mission was, at various times, illegal. In some colonies,
Virginia for instance, the offspring of a white woman and
a Negro slave became free at the age of thirty-one. And
some indulgent masters permitted slaves to raise things for
themselves and sell them or to hire out their scant free time
to gain money to buy their freedom.

The South feared the free Negro, who was generally
more intelligent and enterprising than his enslaved brethren, and the lower-class southerners hated him. Other than
the priceless boon of freedom, and the right to keep what
he earned, he had little advantage over the slave. He could
not vote, could not hold civil office, could not serve in the
militia except as a laborer, could not own a white servant
or marry a white woman. His activities were closely re-
stricted. He had to be very careful in consorting with

slaves—there was the ever present fear of insurrection plots. There was only one thing he could do the same as any white man. None of the restrictions relieved him from the obligation to pay taxes.

The free Negro could also own Negro slaves, and there are a few instances, very few, of Negroes who became wealthy planters. Tradition has it that these were invariably the cruelest masters, but there is no factual basis for this legend. In fairness to the South it should be said that the free Negro was little better off in the North. Slave or free, not only did the Negro have no civil rights, he had very few of the human rights about which his white brothers in America were starting to make such a fuss.

The last quarter of the eighteenth century and the early years of the nineteenth brought a great change in the attitude toward slavery. During the first half of this period it came within a whisker of being so curbed that it would inevitably have died out peacefully. By the end of the period it had become so firmly entrenched in the South and had become so intertwined with economics and politics that there was faint hope that it would disappear without conflict—at least for many years.

In this era liberal ideas were sweeping both the New and the Old Worlds—ideas which would result in parliamentary reforms in England and revolutions in France and in North and South America. Liberty and freedom were magic words, and some of this emotional concern for the rights of man reflected for the benefit of the Negro—some, not much.

In 1772 Virginia passed thirty-three acts to restrict slavery by prohibiting the further importation of slaves. They were all annulled by George III. This led Thomas Jefferson, four years later, to include in the first draft of the

Declaration of Independence the charge that the King has "waged cruel war against human nature itself, violating its most sacred rights of life and liberty in the persons of a distant people who never offended him, captivating and carrying them into slavery in another hemisphere, or to incur miserable death in their transportation thereto." The Continental Congress removed this charge from the Declaration, "in compliance," wrote Jefferson, "to South Carolina and Georgia," and he added that there were some northern people who objected to his condemnation of slavery because, though they had few slaves themselves, they "had been pretty considerable carriers of them to others."

The first antislavery society was established in 1774 by the Quakers in Philadelphia, with non-Quaker Benjamin Franklin as its president. Franklin's last public paper, written on his deathbed, was a condemnation of slavery. It was another hoax which purported to be a conversation with the Dey of Algiers in which the ruler advanced every argument that the proslavery people were using to justify Negro slavery. In the fictitious interview the Dey sought to prove that Christian slaves were necessary for the economy of Algiers and that the Christians whom he had enslaved were much better off under his humane ownership than they had been as free men.

In 1784 Thomas Jefferson authored an effort to contain slavery within its existing boundaries. At the end of the Revolution the original states ceded to the federal government their claims to lands beyond the mountains—the broad belt between the Appalachians and the Mississippi, stretching from the Great Lakes to the Gulf. It was proposed to carve this territory into seventeen states. Jefferson presented to the Continental Congress an ordinance listing five conditions under which these new states would be admitted to the Union. The fifth condition was, "After the year of the Christian era 1800, there shall be neither slavery nor involuntary servitude in any of these states, otherwise than in the punishment of crime, whereof the party shall have been duly convicted."

The antislavery clause was stricken out by the Congress, although sixteen delegates voted for it and only seven against. This bizarre result was possible because of a unit rule in the Continental Congress under which each state had one vote. The majority of the antislavery delegates did not control the votes of a majority of the states. Had Jefferson's provision been carried, slavery would have been prohibited in the future states of Kentucky, Tennessee, Alabama and Mississippi, which were part of this territory. In 1787 Congress passed the Northwest Ordinance, which was essentially the same bill that Jefferson had drawn three years earlier, including the antislavery clause. But the Northwest Ordinance applied to territory only north of the Ohio River, from which the free states of Ohio, Indiana, Illinois, Michigan and Wisconsin would be carved. Four years after the Revolution, and before the new country had its permanent government, slavery was starting to create the rift between the North and the South.

At the end of the Revolution the northern states started to abolish slavery, led by Massachusetts in 1783. Massachusetts' claim to leadership is challenged by Vermont, whose constitution, adopted in 1777, prohibited slavery; but Vermont did not become a state until 1791. If one wants to split a hair very finely, Georgia can be listed as the first free colony. When it was founded in 1733 its charter forbade slavery. This lasted until 1749 when the Georgia planters, envious of the prosperity of their slaveowning

South Carolina neighbors, convinced the authorities that "the one thing needful for the welfare of the colony is slavery."

By 1804 all of the northern states had emancipated their slaves; some outright, others gradually. In the meantime Kentucky and Tennessee had entered the Union as slave states and Ohio as a free state. The line-up then stood eight states slave and nine states free.

When the delegates to the Constitutional Convention sat down in 1787 to develop a better charter of government than the Articles of Confederation they did a masterful job of "weaseling" on slavery. The Constitution of the United States clearly endorses slavery, but the words "slave" and "slavery" do not appear in the document. This, presumably, was a sop to the conscience of some of the delegates. Or, as Abraham Lincoln later theorized, "It was hoped that when it [the Constitution] should be read by intelligent and patriotic men, after the institution of slavery had passed from among us, there would be nothing on the face of the great charter of liberty suggesting that such a thing as Negro slavery had ever existed among us. They expected and intended that it should be put in the course of ultimate extinction."

Two of the three compromises which made it possible for the convention to agree on a Constitution involved slavery. Although not a part of the compromise which gave the small states equal representation in the Senate, it did affect representation in the lower house. This was to be by population. The South said all population. The North said free population. It was finally agreed that a slave was three fifths of a person and Article I, Section 2, of the Constitution says: "Representatives and direct taxes shall be apportioned among the several states which may be included within this union, according to their respective numbers, which shall be determined by adding to the whole number of free persons, including those bound to service for a term of years, and excluding Indians not taxed, three fifths of all other persons." Anyone owning 49,999 slaves would be a one-man congressional district.

The maritime North wanted Congress to have wide powers to enact navigation laws. The agricultural South did not particularly care but they traded their approval for twenty years continuation of the slave trade in Article I, Section 9: "The migration of importation of such persons as any of the states now existing may think proper to admit, shall not be prohibited by the Congress prior to the year 1808; but a tax or duty may be imposed on such importation, not exceeding ten dollars for each person." The Constitution not only endorsed the slave trade but sought to profit from it.

The third constitutional reference to slavery is in Article IV, Section 2: "No person held to service or labor in one state, under the laws thereof, escaping into another shall, in consequence of any law or regulation therein, be discharged from such service or labor, but shall be delivered up on claim of the party to whom such service or labor is due." This would become the basis of the Fugitive Slave Law.

It is a strange paradox that while southern delegates to the Constitutional Convention were insisting on clauses that would sanction slavery, most enlightened southern leaders were seeking some means of letting go of this bear whose tail the South had inadvertently grasped. Daniel Webster said that these southern leaders considered slavery "an evil, a blight, a scourge and a curse," and that there were no terms of condemnation of slavery "so vehement in the North at that day as in the South."

Four of the first five Presidents of the United States were southerners. They all repeatedly condemned slavery—but they all owned slaves. Washington said, of slavery, "There is not a man living who wishes more sincerely than I do to see a plan adopted for the abolition of it." Jefferson campaigned against the evil all his days and lived with the "hope that a way is preparing for the deliverance of these our brethren when the measure of their tears is full. . . . Nothing is more certainly written in the book of fate than that this people shall be free."

James Madison, who has been called the Father of the Constitution, sadly proclaimed, "It is wrong to admit in the Constitution the idea that there can be property in man." James Monroe added, "We have found that this evil has preyed upon the very vitals of the union and has been prejudicial to all the states in which it has existed."

The conflict between the words and the actions of these prominent slaveowners seems incomprehensible. Surely these great men were not hypocrites. They were sincere when they condemned slavery as immoral and evil. Why, then, did they own slaves? The answer is simply that they did not know what else to do with the Negroes. In their particular cases the slaves whom they owned were better off than they would have been, at that time and in that place, under any other condition that their masters could have devised.

Consider Thomas Jefferson. He farmed up to 5,000 acres in several parcels throughout Virginia with about 500 slaves. Except for those at Monticello he seldom saw most of them. Those on outlying plantations were handled by overseers who frequently complained that they could not get satisfactory production under Jefferson's rules for humane treatment of labor. The illiterate field workers knew no other way of life. They worked, and master provided for them. Had Jefferson freed them it is probable that the more responsible ones might have stayed and worked for wages, but many, who had never been conditioned to taking care of themselves, would have wandered off to steal or starve or to be victimized by the first unscrupulous white man whose path they crossed.

These were Jefferson's "people"—that is what he called them. His account books show expenses for the family at Monticello, and the "family" included the thirty-two house slaves. He deplored the situation that made them slaves, but he felt a keen responsibility to them as human beings. Actually Jefferson's slaves were an albatross around his neck—and this was true of many planters. The third President died bankrupt, partly from the cost of maintaining a regiment of inefficient labor whom he was too humane to drive or dispose of.

As the end of the eighteenth century approached, slavery seemed to be headed for early extinction. Despite its sanction in the Constitution, most thinking men, North and South, sought a way to eliminate it. This was partly due to the liberal ideas of the Revolutionary period. But economics was a more important factor. It has been cynically said that slavery always became morally wrong when it became unprofitable. And it was becoming unprofitable.

There were too many slaves. They were still trickling in from Africa and the West Indies despite some state laws prohibiting their import. And although infant mortality was ghastly—perhaps over 50 per cent—the native slave population was growing. The first national census taken in 1790 recorded 757,897 Negroes, 19.3 per cent of the population. The percentage of Negroes to whites has never since been so high. The need for labor was not keeping pace with the growing supply.

It was a simple matter for the North to solve this problem by merely freeing the slaves and letting them shift for themselves—or selling them South before the law went into effect. The few who remained in the North could be absorbed into the economy as free labor. Negro slavery had never worked well in the North. Climate was against it. There were no mass agricultural operations, and the newly imported Negro was less suited to industrial production than the white immigrant—and more expensive. Most northerners owned slaves for prestige rather than practicality. A black coachman was a status symbol, like a mink coat or a Cadillac convertible. But for the South with its great mass of slaves there was no such simple solution.

Much of the agitation to abolish slavery came from southern leaders. Most of them wanted to do something about it—but nobody could agree what to do. A favorite theme, from this era until the end of slavery, was colonization outside of the United States, preferably in Africa. Thomas Jefferson proposed a plan for colonization in 1776, as did Abraham Lincoln eighty-five years later. A Colonization Society was formed. Virginians James Madison and James Monroe were two of its presidents. Virginia, Georgia, Maryland and Tennessee all passed legislation favoring colonization. The general idea was that free Negroes would go to Liberia and that slaves who were willing to go would be freed. The idea never worked. Not many Negroes wanted to go to Liberia.

The extent of southern concern for the slavery problem is indicated by some unusual statistics. In the early nineteenth century 44 of the 57 branches of the Colonization

Society were in the South; and of the 143 Emancipation Societies in the United States, 103 were in slaveholding states.

Suddenly the whole situation was changed by a young Yale graduate from New Haven. It has been said that Eli Whitney caused the Civil War by inventing the cotton gin. This is certainly an oversimplification, but the agricultural revolution which resulted from Whitney's machine prevented the peaceful abolition of slavery.

Whitney's invention was perfectly timed. A few years before, several English inventors had perfected machinery for spinning cotton. In 1790, two years before Whitney invented the gin, a clever apprentice had come from England with the designs of the new machinery in his head and set up America's first cotton mill in Pawtucket, Rhode Island—the first real factory in the United States. New England and old England were avid for cotton. The South had the land, the labor and the climate to meet the need. With Whitney's tool to do the work of a hundred hands in separating the seeds from the fibers in short staple cotton, the South could pour out an avalanche of soft White Gold. The era of King Cotton dawned, and with it the final period of slavery, which the South soon considered absolutely essential to its new prosperity.

Within a decade the slave labor surplus started to become a critical labor shortage. Slave prices skyrocketed. A field hand who sold for $300 in 1790 brought $450 in 1800, $750 in 1845, $1,200 in 1853 and up to $1,600 by the beginning of the war. The slave population of Alabama doubled in ten years. That of Mississippi quintupled in twenty. In 1791 cotton production totaled 9,000 bales. By 1831 it was 1,000,000 bales. By the beginning of the Civil

War it had increased a thousandfold since Revolutionary days.

In 1808 Congress finally outlawed the African slave trade, but this had little effect except to increase slave prices. As with all other aspects of slavery, Congress weaseled by refusing to join with Great Britain, France and Sweden in an agreement to consider slavers as "pirates, felons and robbers." American ships could not be searched by foreign ships, so the favorite flag on slavers was the Stars and Stripes.

The horrors of the slave trade have been well documented. During a voyage it was not unusual for a slaver to lose 50 per cent of the frightened wretches who were chained and packed spoon fashion between decks with a three- or four-foot clearance. But inhuman as it was there were those who would invest in it—most of them northerners, and pious ones at that. There were captains who were bestial enough to command slavers, and although most sailors would rather starve than serve on a slave ship, there were enough who would not to keep the traffic going and growing. The lure of gold was irresistible. A vessel that cost $30,000 could earn $100,000 in a single voyage.

King Cotton brought great changes not only to the South but within the South. Not all of the South was cotton country. The cotton belt stretched from Georgia across Alabama and Mississippi and Arkansas and, after the Louisiana Purchase, into Louisiana and finally Texas. In this virgin territory short staple cotton could be grown almost as easily as weeds. It became the practice for big planters to secure vast tracts of land and clear it with gangs of five hundred to a thousand slaves, who were then set to planting, chopping, weeding and picking cotton on a mass production basis. Between crops the slaves cleared more land to replace that which the ignorant southern planter soon wore out. It might be remarked in passing that the southern planter was one of the most inefficient farmers in the history of agriculture.

In the early stages of this process the Indians suffered more than the Negroes. Much of this land belonged to the Cherokees, Choctaws, Creeks and Chickasaws, with whom the government had made solemn treaties guaranteeing their rights. But the treaties were made when the land was considered worthless. Now that it would produce White Gold it was a simple matter to charge the Indians with "an attempt to establish an independent government" and drive them to reservations in the West. (Where, ironically, some of their descendants have become millionaires from the Black Gold of oil wells.)

The northern tier of slave states was not part of the dominion of King Cotton. Delaware, Maryland, Virginia, Kentucky and Tennessee were not cotton country. But they were not left entirely out in the cold by the new economy. A new form of livestock business developed in the northern slave states—breeding humans. As slave prices spiraled upward it became profitable to raise slaves for the market. Virginia realized a sizable share of its income by shipping 6,000 a year southward; and there were more slave dealers in Kentucky than mule dealers. Washington, D.C., was a port of debarkation for slave brigs hauling cargoes of blacks to New Orleans, and slave barracoons lined the shore of the Potomac almost in the shadow of the nation's capital.

By the 1820s the social, economic and cultural pattern of slavery had crystallized in the form which it would retain until the end. The slave and the slaveowner and their relationship to each other have been described in many

ways, depending on the writer's point of view or the extent of his observations. One observer commented that
some slaves on an Ohio River steamboat on which they
were being taken South for sale were "the most cheerful
and apparently happy people on board." The comment is
interesting because of the man who made it—Abraham
Lincoln.

At one extreme is the picture of the slaveowner as a
heartless brute who whipped a slave nearly to death every
day for sadistic pleasure. At the other extreme is the mistress who is described as sitting up all night in the slave
quarters to nurse a sick child. On the one hand, the slave
is presented as a shiftless, sullen brute who differed from
the ape only to the extent that he could articulate some
scarcely intelligent words. At the other extreme the slave
is pictured as the Aunt Jemima-type mammy, loving and
beloved by massa and missus and all the children—the
sage power behind the throne in the household.

All of these extremes probably existed—but they certainly were not typical. There were probably the same
percentage of brutes and sadists among nonslaveowners as
among slaveowners. But slavery gave free opportunity to
expression of the baser passions. It was, at best, a brutal
business. Thomas Jefferson elaborated on this in one of
his earliest diatribes against slavery:

"There must doubtless be an unhappy influence on the
manners of our people produced by the existence of slavery among us. The whole commerce between master and
slave is a perpetual exercise of the most boisterous passions,
the most unremitting despotism on the one part and degrading submissions on the other. . . . The man must be a
prodigy who can retain his manners and morals unde-
praved by such circumstances. . . . With the morals of the

people, their industry also is destroyed. For in a warm climate, no man will labor for himself who can make another labor for him. This is so true that of the proprietors of slaves a very small proportion indeed are ever seen to labor."

The workday of the field hand started with the dawn and a cold breakfast. He worked steadily until noon, ate lunch, had a one- to two-hour siesta and worked until sundown. Women and adolescent children were included in the field gang. After work the gang returned to quarters, cooked their own dinners and slept. It was a common custom for slaves on most plantations to get up at 2:00 or 3:00 A.M. and fix themselves another meal.

The workweek was generally five and a half days, with Saturday afternoon and Sunday off. Slaves were not allowed to leave the area of their quarters after dark, although a lucky one might get a pass to visit a wife on a nearby plantation or to go to town. The roads were patrolled by white volunteers, and a slave picked up without a pass was whipped by the road patrol and then returned to his owner for further punishment.

Slave quarters were rows of hunts of logs, slab or, rarely, brick. All had fireplaces, some had unglazed, shuttered window openings, and they usually had dirt floors. There were no sanitary facilities. The huts were generally somewhat smaller than a two-car garage and housed up to six adults; plus small children. There was absolutely no privacy.

Clothing consisted of a homespun shift and a bandanna for women, pants and a shirt for men. Rations varied with the place and the generosity of the owner, but food was the best aspect of the slave's miserable life. Meat and meal— "hog and hominy"—were issued in amounts ranging from reasonable to abundant and usually supplemented by molasses and sometimes milk. On most plantations slaves were permitted to raise vegetables or chickens for their own use. When millions of free peasants starved to death in Ireland in the 1840s advocates of slavery pointed out that no slave had ever starved in the United States.

Singing and dancing around a fire were usually permitted in the evening, and most plantations had one or more fiddles or banjoes. Generally, drums were prohibited; the white man seemed to connect the drum with wild African tribesmen and signaling that might send messages of insurrection.

In many respects the daily life of the field slave was as good or better than the life of the Irish immigrant laboring on the railroad up North. The work was as hard and as long for one as the other. The Irishman's living conditions were no better and his food probably not as good. True, he could trade his week's wages for whiskey on Saturday night and forget his misery for a few hours; but the slave had the opposing consolation of some family life and an association between the sexes. The difference was that the Irishman's sorry lot might be temporary—the slave's was for life. And, for the slave, there was the whip.

Most managers of slave labor maintained that they could not be worked without a whip. Since they had absolutely no incentive to work except fear, this might well be true. On larger plantations the actual supervisor of labor was an overseer. He might be a humane man or he might be a brute, but his compensation was partially based on production, and he had a personal incentive to keep the gang moving. He applied the whip as he saw fit to this end.

Flogging was the punishment for any offense from stealing a chicken to attempted escape, although incorrigibles were sometimes branded or had their ears cropped. There were laws controlling the nature and extent of punishment. Alabama, for instance, required the punishment be inflicted "coolly and dispassionately, with a whip to be kept for that purpose. . . . Beating with a stick, the fist or kicking are positively forbidden." Several states did not deem it murder if a slave died under correction.

Much has been written of the brutality involved in the whipping of slaves, and certainly with some justice. But it must be remembered that at the time overseers were carrying whips to secure diligence from their labor, boatswain's mates in the U. S. Navy were carrying "starters" for the same purpose and applying them freely to the backs and buttocks of sailors to make the crew move smartly. At the time that the slaveowner was ordering ten lashes for a slave who stole a pig, the ship's captain was ordering like punishment for the hand who stole a can of paint. Anguished cries rang from students in all schoolhouses where the rod was not spared, and Boston masters who condemned the cruel slaveowner, regularly—and legally—whipped their own apprentices. The whip was a product of the times rather than of slavery, but in slavery it was a further symbol of degradation.

The usual formula for operating a large plantation was 100 hands to 1,000 acres. A hand was an able-bodied male or female Negro. Older or weaker slaves, teen-agers and children who worked in the fields were rated as half or quarter hands. In addition there were children too young to work, old people to take care of them, artisans and house servants. To provide 100 field hands a plantation owner might own 250 slaves, all of whom had to be fed. Approximately half of the land had to be used to grow produce to feed the plantation, unless the planter was too shiftless to grow his own feed and bought it, as many did, from the West.

Because he had no incentive to produce, the slave was a poor worker. One Virginian who moved North said that a white farm hand in New Jersey did as much work as he expected to get from four slaves. In all, farming with massed gangs of slaves was one of the most inefficient systems known to history. It was possible only because there was ample, cheap, virgin land. William Byrd of Virginia described the system best by saying that slaves "are even with their masters and make him but indifferent crops, so that he gets nothing by his injustice but the scandal of it."

When William Thackeray visited America and stayed at a plantation house in the South he commented that slavery was "the dearest institution that can be devised . . . fifteen Negroes doing the work which John, the cook, the housemaid and the help do perfectly in your own comfortable London home. And these are the pick of a family of some eighty or ninety. Twenty are too sick or too old to work . . . twenty are too clumsy; twenty are too young, and have to be watched and nursed by ten more."

The big plantation was a symbol of the South, but it was not typical. In 1850 only 2,300 southerners owned more than 100 slaves each. In 1860 most of the South's 4,000,000 slaves were owned by small farmers, each of whom possessed, on the average, less than 10 Negroes of all ages. One population census lists 350,000 slaveholders in the South and 6,000,000 nonslaveholders. Other estimates vary; but it is certain that at least two thirds of the whites in the South, at the beginning of the Civil War, had nothing to do with slavery.

This was the "peculiar institution" which would become—in popular opinion, if not in fact—a principal cause
of the War between the States. It is very questionable
whether, under any conditions, it benefited anybody, although the ruling class of the South claimed that without
it southern economy would collapse. If it did have any
economic value to some slaveowners, they were a very,
very small minority of those who would die to defend it.

One of the summaries of the South's "peculiar institution" was written by George Washington Williams, a
Negro historian who wrote, in 1883, a *History of the Negro Race in America*. Mr. Williams said: "Virginia was
the mother of slavery as well as 'the mother of Presidents.'
Unfortunate for her, unfortunate for the other colonies,
and thrice unfortunate for the poor colored people, who
from 1619 to 1863 yielded their liberty, their toil—unrequited—their bodies and intellects to an institution that
ground them to powder. No event in the history of North
America has carried with it to its last analysis such terrible
forces. It touched the brightest features of social life, and
they faded under the contact of its poisonous breath. It
affected legislation, local and national; it made and destroyed statesmen; it prostrated and bullied honest public
sentiment; it strangled the voice of the press, and awed
the pulpit into silent acquiescene; it organized the judiciary
of states, and wrote decisions for judges; it gave states their
political being, and afterwards dragged them by the fore-
hair through the stormy sea of civil war; laid the parricidal
fingers of Treason against the fair throat of liberty—and
through all time to come no event will be more sincerely
deplored than the introduction of slavery into the colony
of Virginia during the last days of the month of August
in the year 1619."

The Pros and the Antis

And Noah awoke from his wine, and knew what his younger
son had done unto him.
And he said, Cursed *be* Canaan; a servant of servants shall
he be unto his brethren.
And he said, Blessed *be* the Lord God of Shem; and Canaan
shall be his servant.
God shall enlarge Japeth, and he shall dwell in the tents of
Shem; and Canaan shall be his servant.

So went the favorite Bible lesson of southern clergymen
in the mid-nineteenth century. Here in the Book of Genesis
was proof, they said, that God not only endorsed slavery,
but ordained it. The Bible tells us that from the three
sons of Noah "was the whole earth overspread." Shem,
said the proslavery advocates, was the ancestor of the
Anglo-Saxons and Ham, father of Canaan, was the fore-
father of the Africans. So God had commanded that the

black man should serve the white man until the end of time. It was as simple as that.

Such reasoning seems ridiculous in the mid-twentieth century. But at that time there was still a strong hold-over of the Reformation habit of referring all cases of moral conduct to the Bible. Although the word "slave" appears but twice in the Bible, the word "servant" is frequently used to denote a slave. The Good Book does not expressly condemn slavery, and many quotations can be found—or twisted—to endorse it. Hagar was a slave, "and the angel of the Lord said unto her, Return to thy mistress, and submit thyself under her hands." The New Testament commanded, "Servants, be obedient to them that are your masters according to the flesh, with fear and trembling, in singleness of your heart, as unto Christ." And the Tenth Commandment forbids the coveting of "his man-servant or his maid-servant."

A decided change had taken place in the attitude of southern leaders toward slavery by the second quarter of the nineteenth century. Gone were the liberal ideas of Jefferson, Madison and Monroe. Now the pulpit, the press and the colleges were united in condoning slavery and vocal in defending it. The earlier voices which had sought to at least ameliorate or confine the vicious institution had first slackened and then ceased and were replaced with, first, justification and, then, positive praise of the system.

Frequently, the defenders of slavery were not quite clear as to what they were defending. It was not merely a system for controlling labor, nor an economic pattern or a vested interest in slaves as property. It went deeper than that. Although they seldom expressed it in so many words, what they were really fighting for was a social order and civilization as they knew it—and, particularly, a guarantee of white supremacy in that civilization. This was as important to the nonslaveholder as to the slaveowner, perhaps more important.

Chancellor Harper of the College of South Carolina wrote a long *Pro-slavery Argument* in which he said that slavery was "a universal condition" and that examination of any community showed that "servitude, in some form, is one of its essential constituents." He further queried, "By what right is it that man exercises dominion over the beast in the field? . . . The savage can only be tamed by being enslaved. . . . It is as much the order of nature that men should enslave each other as that animals should prey upon each other."

In addition to Biblical support, the proslavery advocates marshaled arguments from history, from a warped concept of ethnology and on humanitarian grounds. They said that slavery went back to the very roots of society and was "the principal cause of civilization." They quoted Aristotle as approving slavery and attributed to it the prosperity of ancient Rome. They neglected to point out that the ancient civilizations which they praised had all collapsed; nor did they mention that, at the time when they spoke, slavery existed in the Western world only in the southern United States and in Russia.

The southern orators and writers maintained—and believed—that the Negro was inferior to the white man both physically and intellectually. With no knowledge to justify their claims they maintained that the Negro's brain was smaller than the white man's in proportion to weight, that his vocal organs were incapable of articulating white man's speech and that he emitted an animal odor.

All southerners (and most northerners) were convinced that the Negro was intellectually inferior to the white man.

Harper wrote that "none has given evidence of an approach to even mediocrity of intellectual excellence." He ignored completely the accomplishments of the very few Negroes who had any opportunity for intellectual development—men like Benjamin Banneker, a Negro mathematician whose almanac had elicited a letter from Thomas Jefferson saying that "nature has given to our black brethren talents equal to those of other colors of man, and that the appearance of a want of them is owing merely to the degrading condition of their existence both in Africa and America."

It was quite evident that the ignorant slaves were intellectually inferior to their educated masters. It was also evident that they were not inferior to the equally ignorant poor whites. But few in the South made this comparison. It was an axiom of belief, upon which their society was based, that the white man was superior to the black man—and any evidence to the contrary was blindly ignored.

Abraham Lincoln commented on this view of the inferiority of Negroes in his debates with Stephen Douglas by saying, "Those arguments that are made, that the inferior race are to be treated with as much allowance as they are capable of enjoying; that as much is to be done for them as their condition will allow—what are these arguments? They are the arguments that kings have made for enslaving the people in all ages of the world. You will find that all the arguments in favor of kingcraft were of this class; they always bestrode the necks of the people—not that they wanted to do it, but that the people were better off for being ridden. That is their argument and this argument of Judge Douglas is the same old serpent that says, 'You work and I eat, you toil and I will enjoy the fruits of it.' "

This ancient argument that slavery was the best condition for the Negro was perhaps the favorite of the proslavery advocates. Slavery brought the Negro out of savagery into the elevating influences of civilization, from heathendom into the light of salvation. It taught him "habits of regular and patient industry" and gave him the advantage of "intimate personal relations with white people." But, principally, the South used the arguments now being advanced by the proponents of the welfare state. Slavery gave the Negro security. It assured him the necessities of life. It gave him medical care and provided for him in his old age. He did not own his body or soul; he had neither rights nor freedom—but he did have security. And the southern spokesmen pointed out, quite logically, that there has never been a civilization in which the individual could have both freedom and security.

Senator Hammond of South Carolina, son of a Connecticut Yankee, told his colleagues from the North, "The difference between us is that our slaves are hired for life and well compensated; there is no starvation, no begging, no unemployment. Yours are hired by the day, not cared for, and scantily compensated. Why, you meet more beggars in one day, in any single street of the City of New York, than you would meet in a lifetime in the whole South. We do not think that whites should be slaves, either by law or necessity. Our slaves are black, of another and inferior race. . . . They are happy, content, unaspiring, and utterly incapable, from intellectual weakness, ever to give any trouble by their aspirations. Your slaves are white, of your own race; you are brothers of one blood. They are your equals in natural endowment of intellect, and they feel galled by their degradation."

To the slaveholder, slavery meant property—two billion

dollars worth—and, in the words of Lincoln, concern for pocketbook impelled the slaveholder "to insist upon all that will favorably affect its value as property, to demand laws and institutions and a public policy that shall increase and secure its value, and make it durable, lasting and universal. The effect on the minds of the owner is to persuade them that there is no wrong in it." Lincoln continued with one of his little anecdotes about a dissenting minister and an orthodox minister who were arguing a point of theology. The orthodox minister said, "I can't see it so." The dissenter pointed out a passage in the Bible, but his opponent repeated, "I can't see it so." The dissenter pointed to a single word, which the orthodox minister agreed that he could see. Then the dissenter laid a guinea over the word and asked, "Do you see it now?" Lincoln continued, in relation to slaveholders, "Whether the owners of this species of property do really see it as it is, it is not for me to say; but if they do, they see it through two billion dollars, and that is a pretty thick coating."

As the slaveowner saw Negroes as property, the non-slaveowner workers of the South saw Negroes released from slavery as undesirable competition. A mechanic in Mississippi wrote, in 1861, "I am Forty years Old A tinner By Trade. I Raised the First Confederate Flag that I Ever Heard Of in 1851. Notwithstanding the Many Ridicules I Encounter'd I told the Citizens that they would All Be Glad to Rally under Such a Flag Some Day which is at present true." The tinner wrote this letter to establish his right to demand a clause in the Confederate Constitution to exclude Negroes from any employment except in agriculture and domestic service. He wanted to make it illegal for Negroes to compete with white artisans like himself.

As early as 1837 there was not a single Emancipation

Society left in the South. No southerner dared to raise his voice against his section's "peculiar institution." Even the Quakers, who had been the backbone of the early emancipation movement, were silenced. Slaveholders and non-slaveholders, country people and city people, farmers and workmen, artisans and professional men, merchants, scholars and clergymen, all agreed that slavery was right, was necessary, was *good*. The repetition of this theme from many sources had welded the South into a solid unit. An essay which pundit Walter Lippmann wrote to analyze the political process generally can be specifically applied to what happened in the South during the thirty years before the Civil War.

"Since the general opinions of large numbers of persons are almost certain to be a vague and confused medley, action cannot be taken until those opinions have been factored down, canalized, compressed and made uniform. The making of one general will out of a multitude of general wishes . . . consists essentially in the use of symbols which assemble emotions after they have been detached from their ideas. . . . The process, therefore, by which general opinions are brought to co-operation consists in an intensification of feeling and a degradation of significance." The symbol behind which the South was emotionally united was white supremacy—in their minds an essential of their society.

There was no such unity in the North. Most of the people cared nothing about slavery one way or the other. The leadership group in business, although they may not have been individually proslavery, were opposed to any antislavery activity or propaganda. Merchants, manufacturers, bankers and shippers were making money from trade with the South, and they wanted nothing to upset the profitable *status quo.* When Chicago's Cyrus McCormick, of reaper fame, gave $100,000 to a theological seminary a condition of the gift was that the institution's antislavery president be dismissed. In 1835, fifteen hundred of Boston's wealthiest aristocrats called a meeting in Fanueil Hall—New England's "Birthplace of Liberty"—which the press described as one of the largest ever held there. Its purpose was to reassure "our countrymen in the South" that they stood solidly behind the perpetuation of slavery.

One New York businessman frankly expressed the position of his class when he told an antislavery clergyman, "Mr. May, we are not such fools as not to know that slavery is a great evil, a great wrong. But it was consented to by the founders of our Republic. . . . A great portion of the property of the southerners is invested under its sanction; and the business of the North, as well as the South, has become adjusted to it. There are millions upon millions of dollars due from southerners to the merchants and mechanics of this city alone, the payment of which would be jeopardized by any rupture between the North and the South. We cannot afford, sir, to let you and your associates succeed in your endeavor to overthrow slavery. It is not a matter of principle with us. It is a matter of business necessity. We mean, sir, to put you abolitionists down—by fair means if we can, by foul means if we must."

At the other end of the social and economic scale there was a strong anti-Negro feeling among ignorant northern immigrants—a combination of fear and contempt which was born of the same lack of security which motivated the poor whites of the South. As late as 1863, when the ignorant Irish led the draft riots in New York City, their principal targets were the city's Negroes, several of whom were lynched.

Starting in about 1830 a new factor began to make itself felt in the North: the militant abolitionist. In earlier days the emancipation societies had been quiet groups, led by such respectable people as Benjamin Franklin and Chief Justice John Jay. But the men and women who took up the cudgels for the Negroes in the 1830s were a different breed. Most famous of them was William Lloyd Garrison, and their ardor and dedication are indicated by the first editorial that Garrison wrote in his abolitionist newspaper, the *Liberator:*

"Let the Southern oppressors tremble—let their secret abettors tremble—let all the enemies of the persecuted blacks tremble. I *will be* as harsh as truth, and as uncompromising as justice. On this subject, I do not wish to think or speak, or write with moderation. Tell a man whose house is on fire to give a moderate alarm . . . I am in earnest. I will not equivocate. I will not excuse. I will not retreat a single inch. AND I WILL BE HEARD."

The general attitude toward the abolitionists can best be indicated by the story of the "well-dressed mob" which tried to tar and feather Garrison in Boston in 1835. George Thompson, an English abolitionist, was scheduled to speak under Garrison's auspices at the Boston Female Anti-slavery Society. On the morning of the day he was to speak, handbills appeared on the streets of Boston saying: "A purse of one hundred dollars has been raised by a number of patriotic citizens to reward the individual who shall first lay violent hands on Thompson so that he may be brought to the tar kettle before dark."

As the time for the speech approached a mob swirled around the headquarters of the antislavery society. One newspaper said there were between six and ten thousand men. Others put the figure as around five thousand. But all agreed on one point—it was a well-dressed mob, "a broadcloth mob." It contained, according to one paper, "many of our first citizens." One university president smugly maintained that "there had been no mob, the persons assembled having been all gentlemen."

Thompson, very wisely, got out of town, but Garrison was made of sterner stuff. He came to the hall early and calmly went to work in his office. The mayor appeared with a few constables and induced the ladies who had assembled to adjourn. When the mob stormed the building the mayor and some of Garrison's friends convinced him that he should leave by a back window and hide under some boards in a neighboring carpenter shop. Here the mob found him, tied a rope around his waist and started to drag him through the streets toward the commons to tar and feather him and "dye his face and hands black in a manner that would never change from a night Negro color."

A few saner citizens wrested Garrison from the mob and took refuge in City Hall. When the mob surrounded that building the mayor decided to place the abolitionist in Leverett Street jail—presumably for his own protection. The transfer was made in a carriage which narrowly escaped being overturned when some of the mob got a rope around it and tried to pull it over. Beaten and bleeding, and with most of his clothing torn off, Garrison was finally lodged safely in a cell. The great irony took place the next day when Garrison, who had been sitting quietly at his desk when the trouble started, found that he was being held under a warrant which stated that he "did disturb and break the peace of the Commonwealth, and a riot did cause and make, to the terror of the good people of the Commonwealth."

There were antiabolitionist riots in most of the major cities of the North. Some abolitionists fared worse than Garrison. Elijah Lovejoy gave his life for the cause. Lovejoy was the editor of a religious newspaper in St. Louis who defended the right to speak against slavery in his editorials. When he lashed out at a judge who had dismissed the charges against the leaders of a mob which had burned a Negro alive, the citizens of St. Louis decided that he had gone too far, wrecked his plant, threw his press into the Mississippi and chased him out of town.

Lovejoy moved upriver to Alton in free state Illinois and got another press. The people of Alton wanted no such troublemaker in their midst and threw his second press into the river before it was installed. When he procured a third press a mob again sacked the newspaper office and destroyed it. Finally a small group of Lovejoy's supporters took up arms to defend his right to publish an antislavery paper in Illinois. They called a meeting of leading citizens to support Lovejoy. The result was a resolution by the meeting forbidding him to publish. Lovejoy ignored it, and when his fourth press arrived, it was escorted to a strong stone warehouse by sixty armed men. Few of these were abolitionists. Their interest was freedom of the press, not slavery.

Late that night, after most of the defenders had gone home, leaving Lovejoy with about fifteen men, the mob started to gather. Most were drunks from waterfront bars, but one observer commented that, "Merchants, doctors and lawyers and even ministers of the Gospel (heaven save the mark) either egged on the mob or were, at best, coldly indifferent."

The leaders of the mob approached the warehouse and demanded that the press be surrendered. When Lovejoy refused the cry went up, "Kill every damned abolitionist in town." Some of the attackers climbed to the roof of the building and set it aflame. When Lovejoy and two others crawled out to extinguish the blaze they were met by a hail of gunfire from the street. Lovejoy stumbled back into the building to die with five buckshot in his chest. The mob wrecked the press and departed, leaving the body of abolitionism's first martyr on the stone floor. Twenty years later Abraham Lincoln would write, "The madness and pitiless determination with which the mob steadily pursued Lovejoy to his doom marks it as one of the most unreasoning and unreasonable in all time except that which doomed the Savior to the cross."

Northern opposition to the abolitionists in the 1830s and 1840s was strongest in the cities, where the mercantile class was dominant. Most of the eastern colleges opposed them—Harvard dismissed an abolitionist professor from its faculty. When a speaker criticized slavery in a speech at Harvard, Henry Wadsworth Longfellow recorded that he left the hall because "the shouts and hisses and the vulgar interruptions grated on my ears." Although many abolitionist leaders were clergymen, and the movement was basically a religious one, they were not generally supported by the churches. In 1835 not a single church in Boston would permit Garrison to hold a meeting. But the opposition was not based entirely on proslavery sentiments. Most people considered the abolitionists as fanatics and troublemakers—which admittedly many of them were. Ralph Waldo Emerson, himself an abolitionist, described them by writing, "The new race is stiff, heady and rebellious; they are fanatics in freedom."

Most of the abolitionist leaders came from Puritan stock—the majority of them were New Englanders. They were, for the most part, well-educated young professional men—doctors, lawyers, writers, teachers, ministers—whose grandparents had fought in the Revolution. They should have represented the leading class in the community, but by the time their mission took shape this function had been usurped by the "new rich" of the infant industrial era. The abolitionists were outside the mainstream of life. They have been described as "an elite without a function."

They turned to reform in many areas of human activity. Most abolitionists were also involved in other causes—prohibition, prison reform, education for the blind, deaf and dumb, world peace, women's rights, penny postage. They opposed slavery on moral grounds. In their Calvinist concept it was sinful, and sin must be wiped out. Their Puritan ancestors had been concerned with sins of the flesh. The new breed were concerned with the sins of the nation—and the greatest of these was slavery.

Abolitionist leaders whose names are known today gained their fame in other fields. Horace Mann was active in abolitionism as well as public education. Abolitionist Samuel Gridley Howe won reknown for the training of the deaf and blind and Dorothea Dix for improved prison and poorhouse conditions. Among the famed writers of the day, in addition to Emerson, John Greenleaf Whittier, James Russell Lowell and Henry Thoreau were active abolitionists and, to a lesser extent, Henry Wadsworth Longfellow. Whittier's was perhaps the busiest abolitionist pen, producing such poems as *The Farewell of a Virginia Slave Mother:*

> Gone, gone—sold and gone,
> To the rice-swamp dank and lone,
> From Virginia's hills and waters;
> Woe is me, my stolen daughters.

One factor that acted against public acceptance of the abolitionists was the unpopularity of some of their supplementary causes and their unconventional actions. John Humphrey Noyes started the Oneida Community where scientific breeding was to replace conventional marriage. The public condemned it as free love. Garrison dabbled in spiritualism. The Welds pushed health foods on the side. The Tappen brothers, two of the few businessmen in the movement, would not permit chairs in their offices—all business had to be conducted standing up. One abolitionist attended meetings dressed as Father Time, complete with scythe. Another clergyman preached abolition and then took all his clothes off in broad daylight and swam in the Charles River. Abby Folsom, a female abolitionist, was so vocal on the subject that she would not stop talking. At one meeting when three men carried her, still talking, from the hall she called back, "I'm better off than Jesus—he only had one ass to carry him, I have three."

The cause that was most frequently associated with abolition was women's rights, and this did not help the movement. Many men of that day who might have accepted the idea of the emancipation of slaves considered the thought of female equality and woman suffrage as utterly ridiculous. The Massachusetts Association of Congregational Ministers issued a pastoral letter condemning both abolition and women's rights by saying that the "perplexed and agitating subjects which are now common amongst us . . . should not be forced upon any church as matters of debate at the hazard of alienation and division," and that this might "threaten the female character with widespread and permanent injury—the vine usurps the role of the elm."

There were several prominent feminists in the abolitionist movement. Lucy Stone did not help it by insisting that the word "obey" be stricken from the marriage ceremony and that she retain her maiden name in wedlock—nor did Amelia Bloomer by wearing the ridiculous pants that bear her name.

The most radical abolitionists further alienated public opinion by condemning the Union and claiming that there was a "higher law" than the Constitution. Garrison quoted Isaiah on the masthead of his paper by saying "the compact which exists between the North and the South is a covenant with death and an agreement with Hell." He backed this up by publicly burning a copy of the Constitution. Henry Thoreau did not win popularity in his own lifetime by expressing such sentiments as the following:

"The judges and lawyers—simply as such, I mean—and all men of expediency, try this case on a very low and incompetent standard. They consider not whether [it] . . . is right, but whether it is what they call *constitutional*. Is virtue constitutional, or vice? Is equity constitutional, or iniquity? In important and moral vital questions, like this, it is just as impertinent to ask whether a law is constitutional or not, as to ask whether it is profitable or not. . . . The question is, not whether you or your grandfather, seventy years ago, did not enter into an agreement to serve the Devil, and that service is not accordingly now due; but whether you will now, for once and at last, serve God . . . by obeying that eternal and only just CONSTITUTION which He, and not any Jefferson or Adams, has written in your being."

None of the abolitionist fanaticism did the Negro much good. Perhaps the main reason was that the abolitionists insisted on immediate emancipation, regardless of consequences, and maintained that the Negro was the absolute equal of the white man in every respect. In the 1830s and

1840s there were few in the North who would accept this premise.

Two members of the Illinois legislature issued a protest against certain resolutions of that body which said that they "believe that the institution of slavery is founded on both injustice and bad policy, but that the promulgation of abolition doctrines tends rather to increase than abate its evils." One of the two men who signed it was Abraham Lincoln.

The situation was somewhat different in the West. Ohio was a hotbed of antislavery agitation under leaders from Western Reserve College near Cleveland and Oberlin College, which was organized to train both white and Negro students and, more unusual, female students. Oberlin was the first college in America to grant Bachelor of Arts degrees to women. Here the movement was antislavery, rather than abolition. Its proponents were willing to accept gradual emancipation or compensated emancipation. They, too, considered slavery sinful—but they were not fanatical about accepting any practical means to eradicate it. Ultimately they turned to the ballot box. It was this type of activity that finally set the stage for the end of bondage. The newly organized Liberty party gained the balance of power in Ohio and forced an antislavery member into Congress. The Liberty party later gave way to the Free Soil party; one of the foundation blocks of the Republican party.

The most effective propaganda line of the abolitionists— which started in the 1840s and became increasingly potent in the 1850s—was the threat of the Slave Power Conspiracy. At the National Convention of Abolitionists in 1839 the meeting resolved that "the events of the last five or six years leave no room for doubt that the SLAVE POWER is now waging a deliberate and determined war against the liberties of the free states."

It was the contention of the abolitionists that the slave-holding aristocrats of the South, in coalition with the industrial leaders of the North—"The Lords of the Lash and the Lords of the Loom"—were conspiring to dominate the government and extend slavery not only into the territories, but into the northern states, even applying it to white labor. Events of the 1840s gave substance, in the minds of many, to the fear that the South was planning to build a vast empire based on slavery. The annexation of Texas and the Mexican War were cited as proofs of this thesis. The South, said the abolitionists, planned to make slave states of New Mexico and Utah, divide Texas into four slave states, split California into a slave and a free state, and extend their rule into Central America and the Caribbean by taking over Mexico, Cuba and Santo Domingo.

This supposed Slave Power threat turned much of northern labor against slavery. This was not out of any humane concern for the Negro, nor because they considered slavery immoral or sinful. Rather, they were led to believe that the success of the Slave Power plot might impose slavery on white labor. The basic proslavery argument could be used to support this contention. If slavery was the best system for labor, as the South maintained, why should it be limited to Negro labor? The South argued that the laborer was unfitted for self-government. If this was true, did it not follow that the employer should rule the worker, regardless of his color? The abolitionists could quote from southern newspapers such statements as, "The principle of slavery is in itself right and does not depend on difference in complexion"; "Slavery, black or white, is necessary"; "Slavery is the natural state and normal condition of the laboring man, black or white." And such statements were not confined to the South. Such northern papers as the Salem *Register,* the Pittsburg *Post* and the New York *Day Book* expressed the opinion that slavery was a superior labor system.

Labor, at the time, was unorganized and politically immature, but, for what it was worth, labor leaders campaigned under the slogan, "Down with slavery, chattel and wage." When the chips were down in the 1860s, labor would be largely Republican.

Was there, in fact, a Slave Power Conspiracy? Not as a definite plot, but in essence the abolitionists were right. The South was dedicated not only to perpetuating slavery but to extending it at least into the territories and new states—and one prominent southerner loudly bragged that he would someday count his slaves under Bunker Hill.

Antislavery sentiment in the North was again advanced by the Compromise of 1850. This started when Henry Clay introduced in the Senate a series of resolutions designed to settle the mounting differences between the North and South. Clay proposed that California be admitted as a free state; that certain other territories be organized without restriction on slavery; noninterference by Congress with slavery in the District of Columbia; a declaration that Congress had no authority to interfere with the interstate slave trade; and a provision for more effective measures for the return of runaway slaves.

This last proposal led to the Fugitive Slave Act to amend the original act of 1793. This provided for exclusive federal jurisdiction over the apprehension of fugitive slaves. It established special U. S. commissioners who could issue warrants for the arrest of alleged fugitives and orders to return them to their masters. An affidavit by the claimant

was considered as proof of ownership, and Negroes claiming to be freemen were denied jury trials, nor was their
testimony accepted as evidence. Further, the commissioner
received a ten-dollar fee if he issued a certificate restoring
a slave to a supposed owner, but only five dollars if he set
the Negro free. Also, it provided that any bystander had
to assist in apprehending a slave on command of the agents
of the commissioners, and imposed heavy penalties on anyone who helped a runaway slave.

The Fugitive Slave Act was about as popular in the
North in the 1850s as was Prohibition in the 1920s, and
for much the same reason. Thousands of people who did
not care one way or the other about slavery—which was
too far away to concern them—strongly resented a law
which made them criminals if they chose to lift a finger to
help a runaway slave. So they chose to. In Ohio particularly, the law soon became a joke, and no court could find
a jury that would convict anybody under it.

The most famous Fugitive Slave case was that of
Anthony Burns in Boston in 1854. Burns had been picked
up as a fugitive by a U. S. marshal while working in a
clothing store in Boston, and was claimed by a Colonel
Suttle of Virginia. A mob led by abolitionist minister
Thomas Wentworth Higginson almost rescued him by attacking the courthouse but was driven off, with some
bloodshed. The U. S. marshal called for federal troops,
and President Franklin Pierce wired from Washington that
he was to "incur any expense" to enforce the law.

Although Burns was defended by Richard H. Dana,
Jr., author of *Two Years Before the Mast,* the commissioner
ruled that he was to be returned to Virginia. Angry crowds,
estimated at over fifty thousand, swarmed to the city from
the textile mills of outlying towns. Five companies of

United States Marines were called from the Boston Navy Yard, reinforced by two companies of artillery and some cavalry. A Coast Guard cutter was provided to take Burns back to Virginia. The procession, or parade, started from the courthouse led by Marines, next a battery of artillery, then Burns surrounded by forty-five deputy marshals, then more artillery and more Marines. The crowd, shouting "Shame," pressed threateningly against the military. Abolitionist Dr. Henry Bowditch, son of the great mathematician, said, "Twice I saw the troops charge bayonet and once the cavalry charged with drawn swords."

They got Burns back to Virginia—but it cost the government nearly $100,000 to do it. Citizens of Boston quickly raised $1,300 to buy his freedom, and he returned to Boston, where he turned down a lucrative offer from P. T. Barnum to exhibit him at Barnum's Museum, saying, "He wants to show me like a monkey." Burn's only other comment was the wry statement, "There was a lot of folks to see a colored man walk down the street."

The Burns case raised national indignation in the North. Two thousand troops against one lone Negro created a picture of unfair persecution which the people would not stomach. Several states passed laws which made it virtually impossible to enforce the Fugitive Slave Act. After Burns, no other fugitive was ever returned from Massachusetts.

The Fugitive Slave Act gave great impetus to the dramatic operations of the Underground Railroad, a system for helping runaway slaves that went back to pre-revolutionary days. George Washington once complained that certain runaway slaves, some of them his, would probably never be apprehended because some misguided Philadelphia Quakers made a practice of helping them. The Railway was a network of routes through free state territory along which fugitives were helped by antislavery partisans and kindly or adventurous people, either to the security of Canada or far from the dangerous seacoast cities and border country. Houses at convenient distances where fugitives were hidden during the day were called stations. Those who drove or guided them to the next station were conductors. Some of the best conductors were innocent-appearing children. There was no official organization for the Underground Railway, but it functioned effectively for decades, and smuggled knowledge of its many termini was circulated among slaves in the South.

The means of escape were varied and often ingenious. Slave Harry "Box" Brown curled himself in a cramped fetal position in a small packing case in Richmond and had himself shipped by Adams Express to Philadelphia. Ellen Craft, a light-skinned, well-spoken, mulatto lady's maid, dressed as a young southern gentleman and rode boldly North on "the cars," accompanied by her husband posing as her valet. Three unknown Negroes saved their money from odd jobs, hired a coach and bribed a white man to drive them across the line in style. From the seacoast states many escapes were made by boat, including one in which the Negro lashed himself under the bowsprit and rode alternately under and over the water.

Unofficial "President" of the Underground Railway was Quaker Levi Coffin of Newport, Indiana, who helped between two and three thousand slaves on the road to freedom. When charged before a grand jury with aiding fugitive slaves he swore under oath that he had no knowledge of having done so. He admitted assisting many destitute Negroes who came to him for help and said they were slaves; but, he added with true Quaker casuistry, he had only their word for it that they were slaves, and as the word of a slave could not be accepted in court as evidence, he could not be considered guilty. The jury agreed with him.

Most of the Underground agents were abolitionists, Quakers or other antislavery people; but many, particularly in the West, were involved because it was fun, and not too dangerous, to outwit the unpopular slave catchers and defy a law with which they disagreed. Others who cared nothing about slavery helped because of human sympathy for the underdog. But the total result was to increase antislavery feeling.

The most famous runaway slave of all time is a fictional character—Eliza, in Harriet Beecher Stowe's *Uncle Tom's Cabin*. Eliza had a real, anonymous counterpart who crossed the river ice to Ripley, Ohio. Mrs. Stowe heard of the incident and based her famous description of Eliza crossing the ice on it.

Mrs. Stowe's book, published in 1852, is perhaps the most potent piece of propaganda in history, and did more to arouse world-wide antislavery sentiment than all of the abolitionists; not excepting her brother, Henry Ward Beecher, who thrilled his Brooklyn congregation by auctioning a slave girl from his pulpit. When President Lincoln met Mrs. Stowe many years later he is supposed to have said, "Is this the little lady who made the great war?" although the only authority for this is Mrs. Stowe's daughter. Singlehanded, Mrs. Stowe convinced the North that slavery was a moral issue.

Harriet Beecher was the only daughter of Reverend Lyman Beecher, whose seven sons all became ministers. Born in Litchfield, Connecticut, she moved as a young woman to Cincinnati, Ohio, where her father founded a theological society, and Harriet married a theological student, Calvin Stowe. Her only personal contact with slavery was what she could observe from the north shore of the river, in free state Ohio. In 1850 Professor Stowe moved to Bowdoin College, in Maine, and here, while caring for their six children, housewife Harriet wrote her epic. She wrote furiously, completing the entire chapter of the death of Uncle Tom in one sitting. She seriously claimed that she did not really write the book—that she was Divinely inspired.

Mrs. Stowe expressed the premise on which *Uncle Tom* was based in a single sentence in the preface to the foreign edition: "The great mystery which all Christian nations hold in common the *union of God with man* thro' the humanity of Jesus Christ invests human existence with an awful sacredness and in the eye of the true believer in Jesus, he who tramples on the rights of his meanest fellow man, is not only inhuman but sacrilegious—and the worst form of this sacrilege is the institution of *slavery.*"

Carl Sandburg analyzed Uncle Tom and explained the deep spiritual conviction that it carried as follows: "Little Harriet Beecher Stowe had set out to register in the bosoms of millions of other Christians her own shame of Christian civilization in America, and her own cry for martyrdom. A picture of a slave society was what she tried to make in a large panoramic structure, and it had become mixed with a great personal ideal of the Christ Man. Her hero, Uncle Tom, was a black Christ. He embodied all the implications of the saying, 'the meek shall inherit the earth.' He did what he was told to do; his word was trusted by his master; he could suffer grimly and humbly in his belief that Heaven, a world after this one, would take him in and put right all wrongs. . . . It was the story of Judea located south of the Ohio River, with a whipping-post for a Cross, slave owners for Pharisees, ministers and politicians for hypocrites and Pilates, and a cotton plantation for the scene of a Passion Play.

"By the device of dramatizing a black Christ, she led millions of people to believe there were two countries with two cultures in the United States; in one humanity was desecrated; in the other it was held sacred. She became the prophetess of a passionately emotional point of view that south of the Ohio River was a widespread and terrible wrong."

When she wrote her book Mrs. Stowe wondered whether anybody would read it. Within an incredibly short time it had been read in almost every literate home in the North, frequently aloud around a fireplace while salty tears coursed down the cheeks of youngsters, many of whom would march South with bayonets ten years later.

During the last half of the 1850s antislavery feeling in the North grew apace with resentment toward the South for many other reasons. Slavery could always be quoted to prove that, in the parlance of modern westerns, southerners were the "bad guys" and northerners were the "good guys." As emotions were aroused, few saw the situation objectively. An exception to this was Abraham Lincoln, who gave the calmest summary of the situation of the pros and the antis on slavery. After saying that it was a "monstrous injustice," he added:

"Let me say I think I have no prejudice against the southern people. They are just what we would be in their situation. If slavery did not now exist among them, they would not introduce it. If it did now exist among us, we should not instantly give it up. This I believe of the masses North and South. Doubtless there are individuals on both sides who would not hold slaves under any circumstances, and others who would gladly introduce slavery anew if it were out of existence.

"We know that some southern men do free their slaves, go North and become tiptop Abolitionists, while some northern ones go South and become most cruel slave-masters. When southern people tell us they are no more responsible for the origin of slavery than we are, I acknowledge the fact. When it is said that the institution exists, and that it is very difficult to get rid of in any satisfactory way, I can understand and appreciate the saying. I surely will not blame them for not doing what I should not know how to do myself."

3

The War to Free the Slaves?

When Lee and Grant met at Appomattox Court House it ended the Civil War of bayonets and bullets. But one aspect of the war has never ceased—the conflict among historians as to what caused it. Why did Americans south of the Potomac and Ohio rivers fight to the death with Americans north of the rivers? Nobody has given a definitive answer to that question, although the conflict is often called "The War to Free the Slaves."

Was slavery the principle cause of the Civil War? The answer to that depends on "What paper do you read?" Scores, if not hundreds, of eminent historians, North and South, heatedly support widely divergent views. To quote but two in simple sentences, expert James F. Rhodes writes, "Of the American Civil War it may safely be asserted that there was a single cause, slavery." Equally prominent Harold Faulkner says, "Slavery was the surface issue; the real conflict went deeper."

There are proponents for the tariff as a principal cause of sectional difference. The industrial North wanted a high tariff to protect their manufacturers. The agricultural South wanted free trade which would favor the exchange of their produce for European manufactured goods. South Carolina threatened to secede from the union in 1832 in protest against a tariff act—a movement that was quelled, for the time, by President Andrew Jackson, who sent a messenger to "Tell them, if one South Carolina finger is raised in defiance of this government, that I shall come down there; and once I'm there, I'll hang the first man I lay hands on to the first tree I can reach."

Southern nationalism has been advanced by some as the basic cause of conflict. The South had developed a group consciousness which was not in harmony with the industrial society of the North. In fighting for southern independence they were seeking to establish a nation which would preserve their southern culture.

States rights has been selected as the key issue, particularly by many southern writers who claim that the war was fought to defend the type of Union which the Founding Fathers envisioned. Alexander Stephens, vice president of the Confederacy, wrote long after the war that the "whole subject of slavery . . . was, to the seceding states, but a drop in the ocean."

Economic differences as a principle cause of the war is a favored theme of some historians, who view the struggle as a conflict between two organized economic groups— the northern industrial and business interests and the southern planter aristocracy—for the possession of the government of the United States. They quote Jefferson Davis, when he was in the Senate, as accusing his northern colleagues of using slavery as a blind to delude the unwary as to their true purpose. Davis said:

"What do you propose, gentlemen of the Free Soil party? Do you propose to better the condition of the slave? Not at all. What then do you propose? You say you are opposed to the expansion of slavery. . . . Is the slave to be benefited by it? Not at all. It is not humanity that influences you in the position which you occupy before the country. . . . It is that you may have an opportunity of cheating us that you want to limit slave territory within circumscribed bounds. It is that you may have a majority of the United States and convert the government into an engine of northern aggrandizement. It is that your section may grow in power and prosperity upon treasures unjustly taken from the South, like the vampire gorged with the blood which it has secretly sucked from its victim. . . . You desire to weaken the political power of the southern states; and why? Because you want, by an unjust system of legislation, to promote the industry of the New England states, at the expense of the people of the South and their industry."

Some cynical commentators cite the selfish personal ambitions of public men as a contributing cause to the conflict. Northerners Daniel Webster, Stephen Douglas, Franklin Pierce and James Buchanan espoused the southern cause to gain southern support for their Presidential aspirations; in the cases of the last two, successfully. There are those who say that Illinois Senator Stephen Douglas' fervent endorsement of the Compromise of 1850 and the introduction of the Kansas-Nebraska Bill were prompted, at least in part, by his interest in swinging southern support to a central instead of a southern route for a transcontinental railroad with a terminal in Chicago—a project which would have vastly enriched those who possessed land along the right of way.

Perhaps the best short statement on the *causas belli* was made by historian J. G. Randall, who wrote, "If one word or phrase were selected to account for the war, the word would not be slavery, or economic grievance, or states rights, or diverse civilizations. It would have to be such a word as fanaticism." There is a wealth of evidence to support this statement, and much of it deals with the fanaticism associated with slavery.

Politically, the sectional issue of slavery was presumably settled in 1820 by the Missouri Compromise, which admitted Missouri as a slave state and established a demarcation line at latitude 36°30'. North of this all future territory was to be free; south of it, slave. There were those who did not think that the compromise settled anything. Among them was aging Thomas Jefferson, who wrote prophetically of the Missouri Compromise:

"This momentous question, like a fire bell in the night, awakened and filled me with terror. I considered it at once as the death knell of the Union. It is hushed, indeed, for the moment. But this is a reprieve only, not a final sentence. A geographical line, coinciding with a marked principle, moral and political, once conceived and held up to the angry passions of men, will never be obliterated; and every new irritation will mark it deeper and deeper."

For thirty years almost every prominent public leader tried to prove Jefferson wrong and to keep the slavery issue hushed. Perhaps it is not true to say that the federal government during all of this period was proslavery—but it was consistently opposed to antislavery agitation. There were many little instances, like Andrew Jackson's support for postmasters who refused to deliver antislavery mail, which added up to a conspiracy of silence on slavery in Washington. An exception to this was doughty old John Quincy Adams.

Adams hated slavery; had condemned it as "the great and foul stain upon the North American Union." But he was too shrewd politically to openly align himself with the abolitionists. At the time of the Missouri Compromise he wrote, "Oh, but if one man could arise . . . to lay bare in all its nakedness that outrage upon the goodness of God, human slavery, now is the time and this is the occasion upon which such a man could perform his duties of an angel on earth." But during his Presidency from 1824 to 1828 he carefully avoided the slavery issue.

When he was defeated for re-election by Andrew Jackson, who was backed by a coalition of southern and middle states, Adams retired quietly to his home in Massachusetts. Presumably, as with all previous Presidents, his political career was ended. But in 1830 a group of friends induced the sixty-three-year-old ex-President to run for the House of Representatives. For the next eighteen years the nation had the unusual sight, still unique, of a former President serving in the Lower House. Adams was the nation's last public man who was linked to the Revolution. As a boy he had watched the Battle of Bunker Hill.

The ex-President soon became the lonely champion of antislavery sentiment in the House. It happened somewhat by chance. The right to petition Congress is expressly granted in the Constitution. In his maiden speech Adams presented fifteen petitions from Quakers in Pennsylvania praying for the abolition of slavery in the nation's capital. Soon antislavery petitions were flooding to his desk as a result of a campaign organized by John Greenleaf Whittier.

On some days Adams presented as many as fifty petitions, each of which interrupted the business of the House. For six years his colleagues fumed and protested. This constant antislavery agitation was unnerving, provocative and counter to the implied conspiracy of silence on the unpleasant subject. Then, in 1836, the House passed a resolution presented by a South Carolina representative than any antislavery petition would be automatically tabled without being printed or discussed.

This Gag Rule sought to prevent discussion of slavery in the House, but the proslavery people were hard pressed to cope with the old gladiator from Massachusetts. For eight years he fought them almost singlehandedly, keeping the House in bedlam by using every parliamentary trick to sneak in petitions. He found a way to present every petition that was sent to him, including one from Virginia which prayed that John Quincy Adams be dismissed from Congress, which he laid before the body with a straight face.

The more radical abolitionists were impatient with the only champion of their cause in the legislature because he would not push some aspect of the slavery question to a vote. When they insisted that he get a test vote on abolition of slavery in the District of Columbia he replied, "There is in the House of Representatives [a majority] of two to one opposed to the consideration or discussion of the subject." He later said that he could not get five votes to support such a test. In 1839 Adams presented three resolutions aimed at gradual emancipation. They were tabled without being read.

Although the House continued to be proslavery throughout the 1840s, rapid increase in population in the North brought a constantly growing antislavery minority. Also, many members were unhappy with the unconstitutionality of the Gag Rule. Each year it was maintained with a decreasing number of votes until, in 1844, Adams' motion to rescind it finally secured a majority, and it was revoked. In 1848 eighty-one-year-old John Quincy Adams suddenly crumpled in his seat in the House and toppled to the floor. He died two days later. Although he had been a thorn in the side of the House for eighteen years, he had gained the grudging respect of his colleagues as a fighter. It was a southern congressman who stepped forward to his casket and whispered, sadly and fondly, "Good-bye, old man."

In the Senate, the proslavery element had complete control until well into the 1850s. The northern population increase did not affect Senate representation. In 1850 there were fifteen southern slave states and an equal number of northern free states—plus distant free state California. From a practical standpoint nothing could be done in the Senate without the support of the South, and there were several northerners, like Webster of Massachusetts and Douglas of Illinois, who curried southern favor to advance their personal ambitions.

In fighting northern opposition to the Compromise of 1850, Douglas told a crowd, "The time has not yet come when a handful of traitors in our camp can turn the great State of Illinois . . . into a Negro-worshipping, Negro-equality community." When Webster campaigned for the same measure in Massachusetts, Horace Mann said, "Webster is a fallen star—Lucifer descended from Heaven." And Henry Wadsworth Longfellow moaned, "Fallen, fallen, fallen from his high estate." Congressman Robert Toombs of Georgia knew whereof he spoke when he told the House, "Gentlemen, deceive not yourselves, you cannot deceive others. This is a proslavery government."

In a sense, the political situation was comparable to that which exists today, when the basic conflict is between liberals and conservatives rather than Republicans and Democrats. The two political parties of that day, the Whigs and the Democrats, cut across sectional lines, but the conservatives of both parties, mostly older men, supported the *status quo*. They were, first and last, Unionists who opposed the fire-eating secessionists of the South and the radical abolitionists of the North. Under the ever present threat of secession, the northern Unionists would do anything to placate the South.

The executive branch of the government was controlled by the South right down to Lincoln. Until 1850 there were only three northern Presidents—the two Adamses and Martin Van Buren, a Tammany New Yorker who was hand-picked as his successor by Andrew Jackson. The latter, at one time in his checkered career, had been a slave trader. In his inaugural address in 1837 Van Buren said that he was "determined to resist the slighest interference with it [slavery] in the states where it existed."

The Presidents of the 1850s were northerners—Fillmore from New York, Pierce from New Hampshire and Buchanan from Pennsylvania. But they were dependent on southern support for their election, and possible re-election. Abraham Lincoln said that the political conventions were "struggles exclusively among northern men, each trying to outbid the other for the southern vote; the South standing calmly by to finally cry, 'going, going, gone' to the highest bidder. . . . See how it works. If a southern man aspires to be President they choke him down constantly, in order that the glittering prize of the Presidency may be held up on southern terms to the greedy eyes of northern ambition. With this they tempt us and break in upon us."

In the opinion of antislavery men the whole political history of the nineteenth century had been a series of measures to placate the South. Horace Greeley editorialized in the *New York Tribune* at the time of the Compromise of 1850.

" 'Buy Louisiana for us!' said the slaveholders.

" 'With pleasure.' [said Congress]

" 'Now Florida.'

" 'Certainly.'

" 'Next: violate your treaties with the Creeks and Cherokees so as to let us expand our plantations.'

" 'So said, so done.'

" 'Now for Texas.'

" 'You have it.'

" 'Next a third more of Mexico!'

" 'Yours it is.'

" 'Now, break the Missouri Compact, and let slavery wrestle with free labor for the vast region consecrated by that Compact to Freedom!'

" 'Very good, what next?' "

It was generally believed that the Compromise of 1850 would keep the slavery issue under wraps for some time, at least. But in the early 1850s a change started to take place slowly in the Senate. The debate on the Compromise was the last appearance of the triumvirate of great proslavery orators, J. C. Calhoun of South Carolina, Henry Clay of Kentucky and Webster. The latter two died in 1852. Many of the other old, conservative Unionists, North and South, died or retired during the first years of that decade, leaving Stephen Douglas of Illinois as the acknowledged leader of the Unionists.

At about the same time the Free Soil party—named for

their slogan "Free Soil, Free Speech, Free Labor and Free Men"—had gained sufficient power to send two great antislavery fighters to the Senate: Salmon Chase of Ohio and Charles Sumner of Massachusetts. Antisalvery William Seward of New York, Lincoln's future Secretary of State, was already there.

Still, for the first four years of the decade, there was little antislavery agitation in Washington. When Franklin Pierce took office in 1853 he announced, "That this repose is to suffer no shock during my official term if I have the power to avert it, those who placed me here may be assured." A wave of prosperity was sweeping all sections of the country in the beginning of the railroad boom. Cotton prices spiraled upward, the value of the export crop increasing from $60 million to $100 million during the first half of the decade. Slave prices kept pace; and slavery was never so important as an economic factor to the South.

Then, from out of the blue in 1854, Stephen Douglas upset the apple cart with a bill that proposed that new states to be carved from the Nebraska Territory be permitted to enter the Union "with or without slavery." Nebraska was part of the original Louisiana Purchase. It was larger than the thirteen original colonies, and all of it lay north of the Missouri Compromise line. Douglas' bill implied a nullification of the Missouri Compromise, and a southern amendment soon made this official by specifically revoking the old agreement. Another amendment divided the territory into two prospective states, Kansas and Nebraska. With northern Democrats supporting the solid South, the Kansas-Nebraska Bill passed both Houses after prolonged and angry sessions—marked by fist fights on the floor of the House—and was signed by President Pierce.

Indignation, resentment and a certain fear swept the North at this new evidence of the Slave Power Conspiracy. If the Missouri Compromise was annulled, slavery could sweep through all of the Indian country and even into the Oregon Territory—if the southerners got there first—and unite western corn and wheat with southern cotton in an agricultural empire based on slavery.

Mrs. Stowe's book with its emotional and moral condemnation of slavery was at the height of its popularity. Now the action of Congress added reason and fear to the antislavery crusade. At long last some unity started to take shape. The same men who had flocked to Fanueil Hall twenty years earlier to register their support for their countrymen in the South now crowded into the same hall to protest southern aggression. The New England clergy finally presented a united antislavery front in a petition to Congress signed by 3,050 ministers. In the West, indignation was even stronger. The territory involved was western land, not southern land, and the profits from its development were the natural prerogatives of westerners.

One immediate result of the Kansas-Nebraska Bill was the birth of the Republican party. In the summer of 1854 a group of opponents to the Kansas-Nebraska Bill, from all parties—northern Democrats, Whigs and Free-Soilers—met in Jackson, Michigan, to form a new party in that state. Their resolutions—the first Republican platform—stated that slavery was "a moral, social and political evil." They denounced the repeal of the Missouri Compromise and demanded the repeal of the Fugitive Slave Law and the Kansas-Nebraska Bill. They pledged the party to act under the name Republican "against the schemes of an aristocracy the most revolting and the most repressive the earth has ever witnessed."

The Kansas-Nebraska Bill did not make slavery mandatory in the new states. It left the decision to "popular sovereignty." The settlers in each state would decide the question and come into the Union with whatever laws on slavery their state constitutions provided. In point of fact there was no reason to expect an immediate change in the slave-state free-state balance because there was virtually nobody in the Nebraska Territory to vote. It was still entirely Indian country. Cooler heads assumed that Kansas would ultimately be settled by emigrants from neighboring Missouri and would probably go slave; while Nebraska would be occupied by northern settlers as a free state. "Ultimately" came sooner than anyone expected. The Civil War actually started in Kansas in 1856. Five years before the first shot was fired at Fort Sumter over two hundred people died violently in Kansas in armed conflict between the North and the South.

The first settlers in Kansas came from Missouri to found the towns of Kickapoo, Leavenworth and Atchison. But in far-off Massachusetts the abolitionists decided to try to turn "popular sovereignty" against the South and beat them on their own ground. They organized the New England Emigrant Aid Society to provide financial suport for anyone who wanted to homestead in the new territory. Little bands of New Englanders started west, to be swelled along the way by midwestern settlers. They founded the towns of Topeka and Lawrence. Few of them were abolitionists. Most had no interest in slavery as an institution. They wanted to farm virgin land on the western plains. Their only concern with slavery was that they did not want to be controlled by southern slaveholders.

When, in 1855, it came time to put popular sovereignty to the test by electing a legislature and forming a consti-

tution for Kansas there were approximately eight thousand settlers in the territory; well over half of them from
the South. But the southerners took no chances. They
reasoned that anybody who was there on election day was
a citizen of Kansas. When voting time approached, approximately five thousand armed men from the western
counties of Missouri rode across the border to cast their
ballots for proslavery candidates—and to stand at the pol-
ling places with rifle and Bowie knife to discourage any
opposition. Kansas was quickly organized with an entirely
proslavery legislature. It promptly passed "an act to punish
offenses against slave property," which provided the death
penalty for helping a slave to escape and two years at hard
labor for "speaking or writing against slavery."

The northern settlers in Kansas decided that their only
salvation was to declare the election illegal and form their
own government. They met in 1855 and adopted the
"Topeka Constitution," which prohibited slavery. But
they were as much anti-Negro as they were antislavery.
Along with the constitution went an ordinance prohibiting the entrance of Negroes, slave or free, into the state.
By the end of 1855 there were two separate governments
in Kansas, one slave, the other free—both applying for admission of the state into the Union.

Southerners were indignant at the invasion of what they
now considered their rightful territory by the northern
emigrants, and the tough and aggressive Missourians took
drastic action. The proslavery Kansas militia, known by
the engaging name of the "Kickapoo Rangers," reinforced
by bands of "Border Ruffians" from Missouri, attacked the
antislavery town of Lawrence, sacked the place and burned
the hotel and newspaper.

At first the northern settlers were at a distinct disadvantage. Those who had come to till the soil were mostly peaceful people, unlike the many rough adventurers who raided across the line from Missouri. Later, the antislavery faction would be reinforced by men who differed from the "Border Ruffians" only in their objectives. But the salvation of the northerners in the year of savage guerilla fighting that followed the Lawrence raid were their "Beecher Bibles."

Few of the southerners were armed with modern weapons. Most had only muzzle-loading rifles. In the East a new weapon was being made: the Sharps carbine, which could fire from five to ten shots as rapidly as a muzzle-loader could fire one. Calling the new weapon a "truly moral agency," Henry Ward Beecher raised money from his congregation to ship some to the northern settlers. With each carbine he shipped a Bible, and the cases were marked "Books." Hundreds of additional weapons were sent by New England abolitionists, and all were called "Beecher Bibles."

President Pierce did what he could to favor the proslavery forces in the newly settled territory, but the subject of "Bleeding Kansas" threw Congress into a turmoil. In one of his greatest speeches Senator Charles Sumner castigated the southern statesmen in violent terms. His most insulting references were to Stephen Douglas and to Senator Andrew Butler of South Carolina. Douglas was well able to take care of himself in forensic debate and answered in kind, but the general feeling among southerners was that Sumner's speech was an insult to the South.

Two days after the speech a relative of Butler's, South Carolina Congressman Preston Brooks, walked over to the Senate chamber after that body had adjourned and found Sumner writing letters at his desk. With a heavy walking stick he beat the senator insensible before Sumner could get his long legs out from under the desk; injuring him so badly that he was unable to return to the Senate for almost three years. During that critical period before the war his empty chair was a constant reminder to northern senators of the violent hatred which was burning in their southern colleagues. Many congressmen came to the legislative halls armed. The fighting in Kansas petered out late in 1857 when the situation was brought under control by a strong territorial governor, but the territory was not admitted to the Union, as a free state, until 1861.

The next wedge to widen the North-South rift was driven by the Supreme Court. A slave named Dred Scott had been taken by his master from Missouri into the Indian Territory—free soil under the Missouri Compromise, before the Kansas-Nebraska Act. After Scott was taken back to Missouri he sued for his freedom on the grounds that his sojourn in the territory had released him from slavery. When the case reached the Supreme Court that tribunal ruled against Scott. But the decision went much further. The Court gratuitously added that the Missouri Compromise had always been unconstitutional because Congress had no authoritiy to legislate on the subject of slavery in the territories. Chief Justice Roger Taney wrote that "the rights of the Declaration of Independence do not relate to the Negro for whom citizenship is impossible." Both the judicial and executive branches of the federal government took the position that, for all practical purposes, the United States was ruled by the South.

Aside from the political scene, the 1850s were a time of ferment in the North—a decade of crusades, reform movements and many forms of radicalism. There were waves of frenzied public interest in many causes. Temperance had its day, followed by a surge of religious free thinking; and this was followed in turn by a sweep of religious revivalism. Women demanded with great vigor that they be taken seriously as intellectual beings, and conservatives were horrified at the "short-haired women and long-haired men" who campaigned for women's rights. Labor was restive— the first big railroad strike took place in 1857.

A phenomenon of the decade was the "Know-Nothing party." This was a combination secret society and political organization dedicated to aggressively fighting Catholicism —which had expanded tremendously due to Irish and German immigration. The Know-Nothings were also anti-foreign and antislavery—but at the same time anti-Negro. It was a sort of a northern Ku Klux Klan dedicated to white, American Protestants. Its name derived from the secret nature of its organization. When asked about it a member would invariably reply, "I know nothing." While not politically potent in itself, the Know-Nothing party did add strength to the Republicans in 1860.

A manifestation of the 1850s which had a slight bearing on slavery was a minor cultural renaissance of the period. Except for Edgar Allen Poe and James Fenimore Cooper, who preceded this era, most of the early American writers and poets came to flower in this decade. Longfellow wrote *Hiawatha* and *The Courtship of Miles Standish*. Whitman wrote *Leaves of Grass*. Hawthorne wrote *The Scarlet Letter* and *The Marble Fawn*. Thoreau wrote *Walden*. Whittier and Bryant published their first collected poetical works. Lowell, aided by Emerson and Holmes, started *The Atlantic Monthly*, New England's cultural Bible. Most of these writers were antislavery; all of them favored a form of individual democracy with which slavery was inconsistent.

The final dramatic prewar incident of the decade was the

insurrection at Harper's Ferry in 1859. During the Kansas trouble an abolitionist named John Brown had leaped to national prominence by a series of brutal killings of pro-slavery men who had settled along Pottawatomie Creek. Brown had been born in Connecticut in 1800 and spent most of his life working in many places in the North at many trades—at none of which was he successful. He became a radical abolitionist in his youth, and his hatred of slavery went hand in hand with religious fanaticism. By the time he reached Kansas he was a counterpart of a Biblical patriarch whose favorite theme was the Old Testament teaching of "an eye for an eye and a tooth for a tooth."

One of Brown's sons was shot down by Border Ruffians while walking along a road, unarmed. After the attack on Lawrence the old man set out to exact vengeance against the southern settlers. With his four remaining sons and two other companions he watched Lawrence burn and then calmly set out, in the dead of night, to execute a list of pro-slavery men whose names another abolitionist had given him. Years later his sole surviving son, Salmon Brown, wrote this description of the grisly deed:

"Father's little company went back on the road toward Ottawa. Near there was a station where they served meals, I think, from a tent. Anyway they had a grindstone. We then ground all of our swords on the grindstone. When we had finished, old man Tousley in high glee volunteered to haul all of our crowd back in his lumber wagon. We started off with the cheers of the crowd, with their hats in the air, they all knowing the purport of the mission.

"We went to Doyle's first and encountered a number of savage dogs. Old man Tousley went after the dogs with a broadsword and he and my brother Fred soon had them all laid out. The three Doyles were taken out of the house to a point a half mile or so away and were slain with broadswords. Owen Brown cut down one of them and another of the Browns cut down the old man and the other. Old man Doyle's wife gave the Doyles a terrible scoring as they were being taken from the house. She said, 'I told you you would get into trouble for all your devilment; and now you see it has come.'

"Henry Sherman was killed by Henry Thompson, and also Wilkinson, at about the same time the Doyles were. Father never raised a hand in slaying the men. He shot a bullet into the head of old man Doyle about a half hour after he was dead, but what for I do not know. Perhaps it was to call Thompson and Winer so that they could locate us and we could all get together and return to our camp."

John Brown later moved to New England to secure financial support for a fantastic scheme. He proposed to spearhead a slave insurrection by capturing the arsenal at Harper's Ferry, Virginia. When the Negroes flocked to him he would arm them and establish his black army in the fastnesses of the Appalachians at the foundation for a more widespread slave uprising.

Northern abolitionists were eager for the plot, financed Brown's little company and sent Sharps carbines and five hundred pikes to a hide-out he established in Maryland a few miles from the ferry. On the night of October 16, 1859, he led his band of twenty-one men—including three of his sons and five Negroes—across the Potomac and easily captured the armory, the arsenal and the town. He sent men out to bring in two of the area's leading citizens as hostages and a number of their slaves to augment his band.

The next day sniping between Brown's band and local militia resulted in a few casualties on both sides—ironically, the first man slain by the insurrectionists was the free Negro baggage-master of the Baltimore and Ohio Railroad. The militia had little stomach for facing the Sharps of the keen-eyed Kansans, but they did drive Brown's band into the engine house of the arsenal.

Fantastic rumors of the great insurrection at Harper's Ferry swept North and South. There were reports of hundreds or thousands of slaves under arms who were about to extend their revolt throughout Virginia and Maryland. In Washington, Secretary of War John B. Floyd called for Marines from the Navy Yard and sought an officer to command them. Lieutenant Colonel Robert E. Lee was on leave in his home across the Potomac in Arlington—the white-columned mansion which today immediately overlooks the grave of the late President Kennedy. A young cavalry lieutenant was waiting in Floyd's office to try to sell his invention of a new saber attachment. The Secretary sent the South's future great cavalry general Jeb Stuart galloping across the bridge to summon the Confederacy's future Commander-in-Chief. Lee galloped back, in civilian clothes.

Lee, Stuart and the Marines under Lieutenant Israel Green arrived at Harper's Ferry on the night of October 17. Brown's band by this time was reduced to five unwounded followers. No Negroes had flocked to his standard. In fact, those whom he had "freed" when he brought in the hostages had quietly sneaked away, and when it was all over they were found back in their slave quarters. The Negroes were too sensible to become involved in this dangerous and harebrained scheme. Few slaves at this or any other time sought their freedom through bloody insurrection. The Negroes were basically a more peaceable people than their white brethren.

Fearing for the lives of the hostages Lee ordered the Marines to attack at dawn, using only the bayonet. First, he sent Stuart forward with a surrender demand, telling him to wave his hat if it was not accepted. When the gay lieutenant gave the signal twenty-four Marines swept forward, carrying a ladder as a battering ram. On their second thrust it made a hole in the door big enough for Lieutenant Green to crawl through, followed by a Marine paymaster armed only with a swagger stick. Green cut Brown down with his dress sword, wounding the abolitionist superficially. The next Marine through the door was killed, but his comrades quickly bayoneted the only two of Brown's men who were still firing. It was all over three minutes after Stuart had waved his hat.

From a military standpoint Lee considered the affair trifling. In his report he called Brown's band "rioters" rather than insurrectionists and added, "The result proves that the plan was the attempt of a fanatic or a madman." But, in the emotional tension that prevailed it became a *cause célèbre*. Brown and four of his followers were convicted after a showcase trial by the state of Virginia and sentenced to be hung. Fearing an attempt to rescue the prisoners Virginia turned out the cadets of V.M.I. and several crack militia units to guard the execution. Among the thousands who watched old John Brown mount the scaffold on December 2, 1859, was a private in the rear rank of Company F of one of the Richmond militia regiments named John Wilkes Booth.

Brown had refused a southern clergyman, but at least one man prayed for him as the noose was placed around his neck. That night the commander of the V.M.I. cadets, Major Thomas Jonathan Jackson, not yet called "Stonewall," wrote his wife that he prayed for the abolitionist because, "I feared that this man about to die might receive the sentence, 'Depart, ye wicked into the everlasting fire.' "

John Brown, dead, became a symbol to both North and South. To the latter he was a villain of blackest hue, but no worse than those who backed him. Here was evidence, they said, that the North would incite the thing that the South had feared for more than a century—a slave rebellion which would destroy their society, desecrate their women and leave their country in flames.

To the North, Brown was a brave martyr. Horace Greeley's editorial was typical of the outpouring of the northern press and pulpits. He wrote: "Unwise the world would pronounce him—reckless of artificial yet palpable obligations he certainly was; his very errors were heroic, the faults of a brave, impulsive, truthful nature, impatient of wrong and only too conscious that *resistance to tyrants is obedience to God*. Let whoever would cast the first stone ask himself whether his own noblest act was equal in grandeur and nobility to that for which John Brown payed the penalty on the gallows."

John Brown's final words were a prophetic message: "I pity the poor in bondage that have none to help them. . . . I think I did right and that others will do right to interfere at any time. . . . You may dispose of me easily, but this question is still to be settled—this Negro question—the end of that is not yet."

After Brown's death the nation rushed rapidly toward Armageddon, with tempers and tensions drawn taut on both sides. General Winfield Scott said, "A dog fight now might cause the gutters to run with blood." In Georgia, Aleck Stephens explained his avoidance of politics by saying, "When I am on one of two trains coming in opposite directions on a single track, both engines at high speed—and both engineers drunk—I get off at the first station."

But the primary issue was not slavery—at least not in the North. In 1856 the Republicans had campaigned strongly against the extension of the evil and had been beaten by better than two to one for the Presidency and had failed to carry either House. In 1860 they had a rather mild plank in their platform opposing slavery in the territories; but the planks that brought cheers from the floor of the convention were those endorsing free homesteads in the West and a high protective tariff.

The Republicans passed over William Seward as a Presidential candidate largely because he was too rabid on slavery. His chance for the nomination dwindled when he made a speech forecasting an "irrepressible conflict." He said that all attempts at compromise with slavery were "vain and ephemeral" and called for the overthrow "by one decisive blow [of] the betrayers of the Constitution and freedom forever."

This was too strong for public taste. There was a candidate with a milder point of view—a lawyer from Illinois who had been born in the slave state of Kentucky. Unlike Seward or Sumner he did not carry the curse of being labeled an abolitionist. So the Republicans went to the polls with Abraham Lincoln and a platform which advocated the restriction—but not the elimination—of slavery. Even so, the majority of the people voted against Honest Abe. In the popular vote he trailed his two Democratic and one Whig opponent by almost 1,000,000 votes. (The Democrats had split into sectional factions and fielded a northern and a southern candidate.) All of his opponents were running on tickets calling for either an extension of slavery or a retention of the *status quo* and a hands-off policy by the federal government.

As soon as the "Black Republican" President was elected, and more than two months before he took office, South Carolina seceded from the Union, basing its action in part on the election of a President "whose opinions and purposes are hostile to slavery." The seven states which promptly followed South Carolina into a southern confederacy justified their secession on northern aggression against their domestic institutions. The four states of the upper South which seceded later did so because, they said, the federal government was trying to coerce the states.

So the debate goes on—and probably always will. Was the Civil War or the War between the States also "The War to Free the Slaves"? There was one man whose opinion should carry more weight than, perhaps, all others combined. If anybody knew what the war was about Abraham Lincoln should have. On August 22, 1862, one month to the day before he announced a Preliminary Emancipation Proclamation, he wrote that slavery was *not* the issue of the war.

Ardent abolitionist Horace Greeley had long heckled the President because, he claimed, Lincoln did not take a firm antislavery position. He published a letter to Lincoln, as an editorial in the *New York Tribune,* demanding that the President issue a clear-cut statement of policy on the subject. Lincoln replied:

"As to the policy I 'seem to be pursuing,' as you say, I have not meant to leave any one in doubt.

"I would save the Union. I would save it the shortest way under the Constitution. The sooner the national authority can be restored, the nearer the Union will be 'Union as it was.' If there be those who would not save the Union unless they could at the same time save slavery, I do not agree with them. If there be those who would not save the Union unless they could at the same time destroy slavery, I do not agree with them. *My paramount object in this struggle is to save the Union, and is not either to save or to destroy slavery.* If I could save the Union without freeing any slave, I would do it; if I could save it by freeing all the slaves, I would do it; and if I could save it by freeing some and leaving others alone, I would also do that. What I do about slavery and the colored race, I do because I believe it helps to save the Union; and what I forbear, I forbear because I do not believe it would help to save the Union. I shall do less whenever I shall believe what I am doing hurts the cause, and I shall do more whenever I shall believe doing more will help the cause. I shall try to correct errors when shown to be errors, and I shall adopt new views as fast as they shall appear to be true views.

"I have here stated my purpose according to my view of official duty, and I intend no modification of my oft-expressed personal wish that all men everywhere could be free.

Yours,
A. Lincoln"

4

Lincoln and Slavery

A few years ago the oldest member of the Senate, Theodore Green, of Rhode Island, retired after a long lifetime in politics. A reporter, seeking an inspired quotation, asked him, "In your long experience, sir, what is the most important thing that a senator does?" The old man looked at his questioner quizzically for a moment and then replied, "Get elected."

Abraham Lincoln was a great humanitarian—but he was also a great politician. In a democracy—or in this democracy, at least—a man seldom wins election to public office by advocating extremist views. The sincere reformer cannot effectuate his ideals and aspirations until he gets into office; and to accomplish this he must sometimes tell the people not what he sincerely believes but what they want to hear.

Although it may be wrong to class Lincoln with a Webster or a Douglas in terms of personal political ambitions, he was shrewd enough to equivocate on such a controversial issue as slavery. And he was no rigid ideologist. Like most American political leaders he was an opportunist who frequently "played it by ear." He used to say, "My policy is to have no policy." In 1862 he confidentially admitted that the reference to slavery in his famous House Divided Speech was prompted by considerations of practical politics.

Lincoln wrote, including his printed speeches, 50,000 more words than Shakespeare, 150,000 more words than are contained in the Bible, including the *Apocrypha*. And to the million-plus words of his writings must be added additional millions of quoted verbal statements. From this vast mass of wordage Lincoln, like the Bible, can be quoted out of context to support a wide divergence of opinion. For instance, this volume has already quoted a comment of Lincoln's on how happy certain slaves seemed to be. This could be interpreted to mean that he endorsed slavery.

Nothing could be farther from the truth. Lincoln abhorred slavery, but not with the fanaticism of the abolitionist. He called slavery "a moral, social and political evil," but he did not accept the view, held only by extreme radicals in that day, of complete equality between the races. This was not based on a feeling of Negro inferiority. Rather, complete equality was impossible under the conditions which prevailed at that time. Like Thomas Jefferson, he hated slavery, but he did not know what to do about it in practical, political or humanitarian terms.

According to an autobiography which he wrote in 1860 it was the Kansas-Nebraska Bill and the whole subject of the extension of slavery in the territories which turned his interest back to politics. He wrote, referring to himself in the third person, "His profession [law] had almost superseded the thought of politics in his mind, when the repeal of the Missouri Compromise aroused him as he had never been before." This may be taken with a small grain of salt; it is unlikely that the thought of politics was ever out of Lincoln's mind entirely.

Many of Lincoln's pre-Presidential statements on slavery were contained in the famous Lincoln-Douglas debates in 1858 when the two men were campaigning for Douglas' Senate seat. Although the debates were part of a state election campaign, they dealt with national issues—principally, slavery. Lincoln lost the election, but he gained what national recognition he had through the exchange of speeches, and he forced Douglas to take a position on the Dred Scott decision which lost him much southern support. This may have cost the "Little Giant" the Presidency two years later.

Lincoln tried to keep the extension of slavery the main issue and avoid the question of abolition and Negro equality. He favored a middle-of-the-road policy which accepted slavery as it was. In an early speech he said:

"Stand with anybody that stands *right*. Stand with him while he is right, and *part* with him when he goes wrong. Stand *with* the abolitionist in restoring the Missouri Compromise; and stand *against* him when he attempts to repeal the fugitive slave law. In the latter case you stand with the southern disunionist. What of that? You are still right. In both cases you are right. In both cases you oppose the dangerous extremes. . . .

"Our Republican robe is soiled, and trailed in the dust. Let us repurify it. Let us turn and wash it white, in the spirit if not the blood, of the Revolution. Let us turn slavery from its claims of 'moral right,' back upon its existing legal rights, and its arguments of 'necessity.' Let us return it to the position our fathers gave it; and there let it rest in peace."

Douglas quickly put Lincoln on the defensive by claiming that Abe was advocating complete Negro equality. Lincoln denied this, saying, "There is a natural disgust in the minds of nearly all white people, to the idea of an indiscriminate amalgamation of the white and black races; and Judge Douglas evidently is basing his chief hope upon the chances of being able to appropriate the benefit of this disgust to himself. . . . He finds the Republicans insisting that the Declaration of Independence includes *all* men, black as well as white; and forthwith he boldly denies that it includes Negroes at all, and proceeds to argue gravely that all who contend it does, do so only because they want to vote, and eat, and sleep, and marry with Negroes! He will have it that they cannot be consistent else. Now I protest against that counterfeit logic which concludes that, because I do not want a black woman for a slave I must necessarily want her for a wife. I need not have her for either, I can just leave her alone. In some respects she certainly is not my equal; but in her natural right to eat the bread she earns with her own hands without asking leave of any one else, she is my equal, and the equal of all others."

He admitted that the black man was not equal to the white man in all respects, but, he insisted, "in relation to the principle that all men are created equal, let it be as nearly reached as we can. If we cannot give freedom to every creature, let us do nothing that will impose slavery on any other creature."

In one speech he said, "All I ask for the Negro is that, if you do not like him, let him alone. If God gave him but little, that little let him enjoy." And again, as to all men being born equal: "Certainly the Negro is not our equal in color—perhaps not in many other respects; still, in the right to put into his mouth the bread that his own hands have earned, he is the equal of every other man, white or black. In pointing out that more has been given you, you cannot be justified in taking away the little which has been given him."

With characteristic pragmatism he concluded, "I yield to all which follows from necessity. What I most desire would be the separation of the white and black races."

Actually, Lincoln and Douglas did not differ materially on the status of the Negro at that time. The essential difference in their viewpoints was that Douglas was willing to maintain the Negro's inferior position permanently, whereas Lincoln regarded this as an unhappy necessity which troubled his conscience. Like the Virginians among the Founding Fathers he envisioned a future time when the evil of slavery would be eradicated and the Negro would be allowed to develop his capabilities.

The most famous address in the Lincoln-Douglas campaign was the House Divided Speech with which Lincoln accepted the nomination to the Senate at the Republican Convention in Chicago on June 16, 1858. Before the convention Lincoln had read the speech to a dozen of his close political friends. Except for his abolitionist law partner, William Herndon, they all advised him against using the first paragraph, saying it was too radical, "ahead of its time" and a "fool utterance." Lincoln ignored the advice and rose before the convention to say:

"If we could first know where we are, and whither we are tending, we could better judge what to do, and how to do it. We are now far into the fifth year since a policy was initiated with the avowed object and confident promise of putting an end to slavery agitation. Under the operation of that policy, that agitation has not only not ceased, but has constantly augmented. In my opinion, it will not cease until a crisis shall have been reached and passed. A house divided against itself cannot stand. I believe this government cannot endure permanently half slave and half free. I do not expect the Union to be dissolved—I do not expect the house to fall—but I do expect it will cease to be divided. It will become all one thing, or all the other.

"Either the opponents of slavery will arrest the further spread of it, and place it where the public mind shall rest in the belief that it is in the course of ultimate extinction; or its advocates will push it forward till it shall become alike lawful in all the states, old as well as new, North as well as South."

The speech continued to hint at a conspiracy involving Fillmore and Buchanan, Douglas and Chief Justice Taney for the purpose of nationalizing slavery, and struck at the Supreme Court as a dynasty dedicated to slavery from which might come, ere long, "another Supreme Court decision declaring that the Constitution of the United States does not permit a state to exclude slavery from its limits. Such a decision is all slavery now lacks of being alike lawful in all the states."

Although Lincoln had specifically referred to "the further spread" of slavery, and had merely mentioned its ultimate extinction, Douglas pounced on the "house divided" theme as an abolitionist statement and repeatedly quoted the sentence, "I believe that this government cannot endure permanently," to prove that Lincoln favored the enforced abolition of slavery. With some sophistry Lincoln tried to further define his position. He said, "I did not express myself on anything. I simply expressed my expectation. Can Judge Douglas perceive a distinction between a purpose and an expectation? I have often expressed an expectation to die, but I have never expressed a wish to die."

In later speeches Lincoln spent much time in trying to get back nearer the middle of the road. In one speech he said, "Anything that argues me into his idea of perfect social and political equality with the Negro, is but a specious and fantastic arrangement of words, by which a man can prove a horse chestnut to be a chestnut horse. I will say here, while upon this subject, that I have no purpose directly or indirectly to interfere with the institution of slavery in the states where it exists. I believe I have no lawful right to do so, and I have no inclination to do so. I have no purpose to introduce political and social equality between the white and the black races. There is a physical difference between the two, which in my judgment will probably forever forbid their living together upon the footing of perfect equality, and inasmuch as it becomes a necessity that there must be a difference, I, as well as Judge Douglas, am in favor of the race to which I belong having the superior position. I have never said anything to the contrary, but I hold that notwithstanding all this, there is no reason in the world why the Negro is not entitled to all the natural rights enumerated in the Declaration of Independence; the right to life, liberty and the pursuit of happiness. I hold that he is as much entitled to these as the white man. I agree with Judge Douglas he is not my equal in many respects—certainly not in color, perhaps not in moral or intellectual endowment. But in the right to eat the bread, without leave of anybody else, which his own hand earns, *he is my equal and the equal of Judge Douglas, and the equal of every living man.*"

The House Divided Speech continued to haunt Lincoln for several years. In 1862 a delegation of Quakers called at the White House and quoted the "half slave and half free" sentence to prove that Lincoln had then favored emancipation. Lincoln was obviously displeased. He admitted that he had said that and added, "But I said it in connection with other things from which it should not have been separated in an address discussing moral obligations; for this is a case in which the repetition of half a truth, in connection with the remarks just read, produces the effect of a whole falsehood."

At about the same time, when a fellow Republican asked him why he had delivered such a radical speech, Lincoln showed his concern for practical politics by answering, "Well, after you fellows had got me into that mess and began tempting me with offers of the Presidency, I began to think, and I made up my mind that the next President of the United States would need to have a stronger anti-slavery platform than mine. So I concluded to say something."

In one of the debate speeches Lincoln touched on the subject of what to do with the slaves—and admitted that he did not know. He said, "If all earthly power were given me, I should not know what to do, as to the existing institution. My first impulse would be to free all the slaves, and send them to Liberia—to their own native land. But a moment's reflection would convince me, that whatever of high hope (as I think there is) there may be in this, in the long run, its sudden execution is impossible. . . . What then? Free them all, and keep them among us as underlings? Is it quite certain that this betters their condition? I think I would not hold one in slavery, at any rate; yet the point is not clear enough to me to denounce people upon. What next? Free them, and make them politically and socially, our equals? My own feelings will not admit of this; and if mine would, we well know that those of the great mass of white people will not. Whether this feeling accords with justice and sound judgment, is not the sole question, if indeed, it is any part of it. A universal feeling, whether well or ill-founded, cannot be safely disregarded. We can not, then, make them equals. It does seem to me that systems of gradual emancipation might be adopted; but for their tardiness in this, I will not undertake to judge our brethren of the South."

The idea of colonizing Negroes outside of the United States did not die easily. Jefferson first proposed it in 1784 and Lincoln was still proposing it in 1862. It was one aspect of slavery on which there seemed to be some unity of North-South opinion—but this was more apparent than real. Most of the southern opinion which favored colonization saw it as a means of getting rid of free Negroes, not as a form of emancipation. Between 1820 and 1860 approximately twelve thousand Negroes were sent to Liberia, but only about four thousand of these were emancipated for this purpose.

In 1862 Lincoln invited a group of Negro leaders to the White House—the first time in history that Negroes discussed a public issue with the President. Lincoln told them that Congress had made money available to him to promote "the colonization of people of African descent." He tried to sell them the idea by saying, "You and we are different races. We have between us a broader difference than exists between almost any other two races. Whether it is right or wrong I need not discuss; but this physical difference is a great disadvantage to us both, as I think. . . . Your race are suffering, in my judgment, the greatest wrong inflicted on any people. But even when you cease to be slaves, you are yet far removed from being placed on an equality with the white race. . . . The aspiration of men is to enjoy equality with the best when free, but on this broad continent not a single man of your race is made the equal of a single man of ours. . . .

"Go where you are treated the best, and the ban is still upon you. I do not propose to discuss this, but to present it as a fact with which we have to deal. I cannot alter it if I would."

Lincoln continued to describe the war—"our white men cutting one another's throats"—and added, "But for your race among us there could not be war, although many men engaged on either side do not care for you one way or the other. Nevertheless, I repeat, without the institution of slavery, and the colored race as a basis, the war could not have an existence. It is better for us both, therefore, to be separated."

The President then outlined a plan for settling Negroes in a colony in what is now Panama and described the fine farmland, harbors and coal mines of the area. He pleaded with the free Negroes to take the leadership and accused those who would hold back of selfishness. He said, "Could I get a hundred tolerably intelligent men, with their wives and children, and able to 'cut their own fodder,' so to speak? Can I have fifty? If I could find twenty-five ablebodied men. . . . I could make a successful commencement."

There never was a commencement. With the free Negroes, Panama was no more popular than Liberia had been.

After losing the 1858 election to Douglas, Lincoln made several speeches in the East with an eye to the 1860 Presidential nomination. Most famous is one that he delivered at Cooper Union in New York in February, 1860. He

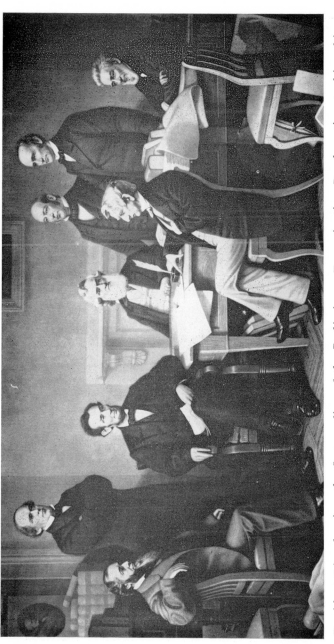

President Lincoln gives the first reading of the Preliminary Emancipation Proclamation to his cabinet on July 22, 1862. Painting by Frank Carpenter.

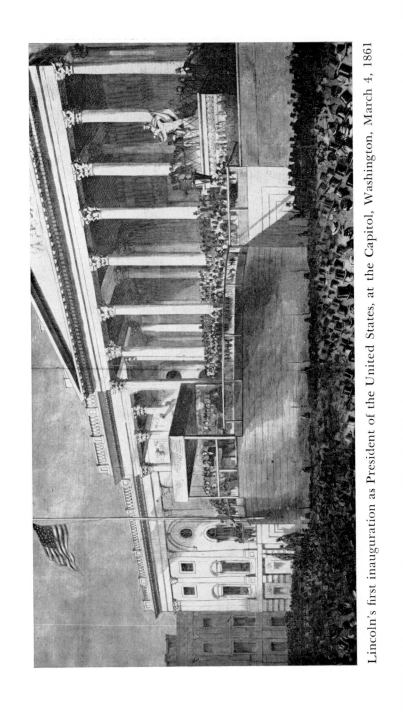

Lincoln's first inauguration as President of the United States, at the Capitol, Washington, March 4, 1861

The south front of the White House at the time of Lincoln's occupancy

Three leaders in the opposition to slavery: left to right, Harriet Beecher Stowe, William Lloyd Garrison and John Brown

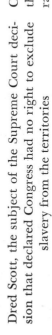

Chief Justice Roger Brooke Taney who wrote in the Dred Scott decision; "The rights of the Declaration of Independence do not relate to the Negro for whom citizenship is impossible."

Dred Scott, the subject of the Supreme Court decision that declared Congress had no right to exclude slavery from the territories

Stephen A. Douglas who opposed Lincoln on the slavery issue

Abraham Lincoln at the time of the Emancipation Proclamation

The first and last page of the Preliminary Emancipation Proclamation issued on September 24, 1862, written here in Lincoln's own hand started by calling the role of the Founding Fathers; the thirty-nine who had signed the Constitution and the seventy-six members of the Congress which had framed the first amendments. He sought to prove that all of these men then endorsed the Republican view of slavery. Then he addressed a few words to the people of the South, although he thought that they would not listen. He said, "The question recurs, what will satisfy them? Simply this: we must not only let them alone, but we must somehow convince them that we do let them alone. . . . Wrong as we think slavery is, we can yet afford to let it alone where it is, because that much is due to necessity arising from its actual presence in the nation; but can we, while our votes will prevent it, allow it to spread into the national territories and to over-run us here in the free states? If our sense of duty forbids this, then let us stand by our duty fearlessly and effectively."

In the election of 1860 Lincoln let his friends campaign for him. Their attitude on slavery was trimmed to meet the public view in the areas where they spoke, but nowhere was emancipation proposed. Lincoln, at home in Springfield, received many letters asking him what he intended to do about slavery if elected. His answers were generally equivocal. To one correspondent he wrote, "Those who will not read or heed what I have already publicly said would not read or heed a repetition of it. If they hear not Moses and the prophets, neither will they be persuaded though one rose from the dead." To another letter he replied, "For the good men of the South—and I regard the majority of them as such—I have no objection to repeat seventy and seven times. But I have bad men to deal with, both North and South; men who are eager for something new upon which to base new misrepresentations; men who would like to frighten me, or at least fix upon me the character of timidity and cowardice."

The South damned Lincoln as an abolitionist. The abolitionists of the North damned him for his middle-of-the-road position, or at best rendered him faint praise. Wendell Phillips, an abolitionist of the Garrison school said, "Let us question Mr. Lincoln. Do you believe, Mr. Abraham Lincoln, that the Negro is your political and social equal, or ought to be? Not a bit of it. Do you believe he should sit on juries? Never. Do you think he should vote? Certainly not. Do you think that, when the Declaration of Independence says, 'All men are created equal,' it intends the political equality of blacks and whites? No, sir. If this be equality, surely Mr. Lincoln's mind is as yet empty. But notwithstanding the emptiness of Mr. Lincoln's mind, I think we shall yet succeed in making this a decent land to live in."

Between his election and inauguration several advisers suggested to Lincoln that he issue a statement as to his position. He replied that he would do it if he knew what kind of statement would influence the South. A declaration that he was not going to interfere with slavery would not do any good, he wrote, although, "I should have no objection to make and repeat the declaration a thousand times, if there were no danger of encouraging bold, bad men to believe they are dealing with one who can be scared into anything."

Before he took office there were two rather mysterious instances which, if taken at face value, would seem to indicate that Lincoln was willing to appease the South by making concessions on slavery. Shortly before his inauguration he wrote to Illinois Republican Senator Lyman Trumbull saying, "Thurlow Weed was with me nearly all day yesterday, and left last night with three short resolutions which I drew up, and which, or the substance of which, I think, would do much good if introduced and unanimously supported by our friends. They do not touch the territorial question."

Thurlow Weed was the Republican boss of New York—which Lincoln had not carried in the election. The letter went on to say that the resolutions should be introduced by Senator Seward of New York if Trumbull and Senator Hamlin of Maine agreed. The first resolution proposed to amend the Constitution so that Congress could not interfere with slavery in the slaves states. The second provided for jury trials for fugitive slaves. The third proposed that northern states should change any state laws which interfered with the execution of the Federal Fugitive Slave Act.

The resolutions were never introduced in Congress, and most expert opinion is that Lincoln never expected them to be. It is assumed that the incident was a gambit on Lincoln's part to strengthen his political position in New York.

The other incident relates to what is known as the Kellogg Compromise. Congressman William Kellogg of Illinois was closer to Lincoln in party matters than anyone except Senator Trumbull. Lincoln had written him, "Entertain no proposition for a compromise in regard to the extension of slavery. The instant you do they have us under again; all of our labor is lost, and sooner or later must be done over." A few weeks later Lincoln had a long, confidential conference with Kellogg. Shortly after this meeting the Illinois congressman introduced a bill providing for a constitutional amendment to legalize slavery in territory south of the Missouri Compromise line. The bill was howled down by radical Republicans. Although Kellogg insisted that he acted on his own authority, there was general belief that Lincoln was behind the maneuver.

The probable explanation of the Kellogg Compromise was that slavery was again being used as a political tool. The Confederacy had already been formed. Kellogg's bill made it possible to say to wavering western Democrats in the border country that if the southern representatives had not left the Congress, a compromise to extend slavery into the territories might have been passed. One shrewd commentator remarked, "Lincoln would like to have God on his side, but he must have Kentucky."

From Kentucky came another compromise proposal by old Senator John Crittenden. This provided that all territory north of the southern boundary of Missouri, running to the Pacific Ocean, would be free soil forever, and all territory south of this boundary would be slave forever, by constitutional amendment. There were many big names in the North that supported the Crittenden Compromise—including Republican Thurlow Weed and August Belmont of New York; Democrat Stephen Douglas and Cyrus McCormack of Illinois. Many powerful newspapers favored it. But Lincoln said, "I am inflexible. I am for no compromise which assists or permits the extension of the institution on soil owned by the nation. . . . As to fugitive slaves, District of Columbia, slave trade among the slave states, and whatever springs of necessity from the fact that the institution is amongst us, I care but little, so what is done be comely and not altogether outrageous."

Two days before Lincoln was to be inaugurated Congress adjourned. Their last piece of business was the passage of a bill to forbid the federal government forever to interfere in any manner with slavery in any slave state and requiring two thirds of the states to approve the measure as an amendment to the Constitution.

On March 4, 1861, Abraham Lincoln delivered an inaugural address which the nation and the world awaited tensely. It dealt with two subjects which were closely intertwined in Lincoln's mind—slavery and the restoration of the Union. Slavery came first. After an opening sentence of greeting Lincoln continued:

"Apprehension seems to exist among the people of the Southern States, that by the accession of a Republican Administration, their property, and their peace and personal security, are to be endangered. There has never been any reasonable cause for such apprehension. Indeed, the most ample evidence to the contrary has all the while existed and been open to their inspection. It is found in nearly all the published speeches of him who now addresses you. I do but quote from one of those speeches when I declare that 'I have no purpose, directly or indirectly, to interfere with the institution of slavery in the states where it exists. I believe I have no lawful right to do so, and I have no inclination to do so.' Those who nominated and elected me did so with full knowledge that I had made this, and many similar declarations, and had never recanted them."

Lincoln next quoted the plank in the Republican platform on which he had run which guaranteed "the right of each state to order and control its own domestic institutions according to its own judgment exclusively." He promised to stand on this plank. He then read the clause of the Constitution upon which the Fugitive Slave Act was based and added: "It is scarcely questioned that this provision was intended by those who made it, for the reclaiming of what we call fugitive slaves; and the intention of the lawgiver is the law. All members of Congress swear their support to the whole Constitution—to this provision as much as to any other. To the proposition, then, that slaves whose cases come within the terms of this clause, 'shall be delivered up,' their oaths are unanimous. Now, if they would make the effort in good temper, could they not, with nearly equal unanimity, frame and pass a law, by means of which to keep good that unanimous oath?

"There is some difference of opinion whether this clause should be enforced by national or by state authority; but surely that difference is not a very material one. If the slave is to be surrendered, it can be of but little consequence to him, or to others, by which authority it is done. And should any one in any case, be content that his oath shall go unkept, on a merely unsubstantial controversy as to *how* it shall be kept?"

Lincoln next turned to the subject of secession and advanced his reasons for believing that "no state upon its own mere motion can lawfully get out of the Union; that resolves and ordinances to that effect are legally void; and that acts of violence, within any state or states, against the authority of the United States, are insurrectionary or revolutionary, according to circumstances.

"I therefore consider that, in view of the Constitution and the laws, the Union is unbroken and to the extent of my ability I shall take care, as the Constitution itself expressly enjoins upon me, that the laws of the Union be faithfully executed in all the states."

He thought that the Union could be restored without violence because, he said, no vital right which was plainly written in the Constitution had been denied to any state or section of the country. It was true that controversy existed in subordinate matters. The Constitution could not be "specifically applicable to every question which may occur in practical administration. No foresight can anticipate, nor any document of reasonable length contain, express provisions for all possible questions. Shall fugitives from labor be surrendered by national or by state authority? The Constitution does not expressly say. *May* Congress prohibit slavery in the territories? The Constitution does not expressly say. *Must* Congress protect slavery in the territories? The Constitution does not expressly say.

"From questions of this class spring all our constitutional controversies, and we divide upon them into majorities and minorities. If the minority will not acquiesce, the majority must, or the government must cease. There is no other alternative, for continuing the government is acquiesence on one side or the other."

Toward the end of his inaugural address, Lincoln returned to the subject of slavery, saying, "One section of our country believes slavery is right, and ought to be extended, while the other believes it is wrong, and ought not to be extended. This is the only substantial dispute. The fugitive slave clause of the Constitution, and the law for the suppression of the foreign slave-trade, are each as well enforced, perhaps as any law can ever be in a community where the moral sense of the people imperfectly supports the law itself. The great body of the people abide by the dry legal obligation in both cases, and a few break over in each. This, I think, cannot be perfectly cured; and it would be worse in both cases after the separation of the sections than before. The foreign slave-trade, now imperfectly suppressed, would be ultimately revived, without restriction, in one section, while fugitive slaves, now only partially surrendered, would not be surrendered at all by the other."

He mentioned a constitutional amendment on slavery and added, "I understand a proposed amendment to the Constitution—which amendment, however, I have not

seen—has passed Congress, to the effect that the federal
government shall never interfere with the domestic institutions of the states, including that of persons held to
service. To avoid misconstruction of what I have said, I
depart from my purpose not to speak of patricular amendments so far as to say that, holding such a provision to
now be implied constitutional law, I have no objection to
its being made express and irrevocable. . . .

"My countrymen, one and all, think calmly and well
upon this whole subject. Nothing valuable can be lost by
taking time. If there be an object to hurry any of you in
hot haste to a step which you would never take deliber-
ately, that object will be frustrated by taking time; but
no good object can be frustrated by it. Such of you as are
now dissatisfied still have the old Constitution unimpaired
and, on the sensitive point, the laws of your own framing
under it; while the new administration will have no immediate power, if it would, to change either. If it were
admitted that you who are dissatisfied hold the right side
in the dispute, there still is no single good reason for
precipitate action. Intelligence, patriotism, Christianity,
and a firm reliance on Him who has never yet forsaken
this favored land, are still competent to adjust in the best
way all our present difficulty.

"In your hands, my dissatisfied fellow-countrymen, and
not in mine, is the momentous issue of civil war. The
government will not assail you. You can have no conflict
without being yourselves the aggressors. *You* have no oath
registered in heaven to destroy the government, while *I*
shall have the most solemn one to 'preserve, protect and
defend it.'

"I am loath to close. We are not enemies, but friends.
We must not be enemies. Though passion may have

strained, it must not break our bonds of affection. The mystic chords of memory, stretching from every battlefield and patriot grave, to every living heart and hearthstone, all over this broad land, will yet swell the chorus of the Union when again touched, as surely they will be, by the better angels of our nature."

So Lincoln took office to preside over "the house divided." Little was expected of the lean, boorish fellow from the backwoods. The South condemned him as an apostle of abolition, which he was not. The abolitionists condemned him as a weakling without the courage of his convictions—if indeed his convictions were not, by their rabid standards, proslavery. Many extremists and moderates alike condemned him for his policy of having no policy.

But there was no reason for anybody not to understand where Lincoln stood on slavery. He believed that it was morally wrong for man to hold his fellow man as property—but he had no intention of freeing the slaves. He was a constitutionalist, and in his view neither he nor the Congress could legally interfere with slavery in the states where it existed. He would not interfere with the slave trade within the slave states. The Fugitive Slave Act was the law of the land. He would enforce it. He was opposed to abolition in the District of Columbia except by popular referendum.

The extension of slavery into the territories was a different matter. This was federal land and Lincoln held that, in the absence of any specific provision in the Constitution regarding slavery in such areas, the federal government had the right to legislate on the subject. And he proposed that such legislation would forbid it. This, and not freedom for the Negroes, was the sole slavery issue.

Partial Freedom

In New Orleans, where he commanded the Union troops
which occupied the city after Farragut captured it, they
called him "Beast" Butler. He had hung, out of hand, a
secessionist who had ripped up an American flag, and some
said that he stole people's silverware; but their main reason for considering him a monster was the order he issued
to the effect that any New Orleans woman who continued
to insult Union soldiers would be treated as "a woman
of the town plying her vocation." The order was harsh,
but there was much provocation. Lincoln later relieved
him from duty in New Orleans, but this was for corruption
rather than beastliness.

Lincoln said that General Benjamin F. Butler reminded
him of "Jim Jett's brother. Jim used to say that his
brother was the damndest scoundrel that ever lived, but
by the infinite mercy of Providence he was also the damndest fool.' But the Beast of New Orleans should have an-

other appellation. He was actually "the man who freed the slaves." At least, he freed the first Negroes who were released from bondage as a result of the war.

Before he went to New Orleans, Butler commanded at Fortress Monroe, Virginia. Late in May, 1861, forty days after Fort Sumter surrendered, three male Negroes sought sanctuary in Butler's camp. Butler put them to work. They were shortly followed by many more, and on May 27 Butler wrote to Commanding General Winfield Scott—a letter which marked, in a sense, the beginning of Negro emancipation. "The question in regard to slave property is becoming one of very serious magnitude. The inhabitants of Virginia are using their Negroes in the batteries, and are preparing to send their women and children South. The escapes from them are very numerous, and a squad has come in this morning and my pickets are bringing in their women and children. . . .

"As a means of offense in the enemy's hands, these Negroes, when able-bodied, are of great importance. Without them, the batteries could not have been erected; at least for many weeks. As a military question, it would seem to be a measure of necessity to deprive their masters of their services.

"How can this be done? As a political question and a question of humanity, can I receive the services of a father and a mother and not take the children? Of the humanitarian aspect, I have no doubt; of the political one, I have no right to judge; I therefore submit all this to your better judgment."

Butler felt that because the slaves were being used to aid the southern war effort, they were legitimate contraband of war and could legally be confiscated like any other war material. The word caught on with the southern Negroes, and slaves were soon flocking to the union lines to proclaim smilingly, "I's contraband."

Scott referred the matter to Secretary of War Simon Cameron, who wrote Butler, "Your action in respect to the Negroes who came within your lines from the service of the rebels is approved. . . .

"While you will permit no interference, by persons under your command, with the relations of persons held to service under the laws of any state, you will, on the other hand, so long as any state within which your military operations are conducted remains under the control of such armed combinations, refrain from surrendering to alleged masters, any persons who come within your lines. You will employ such persons in the services to which they will be best adapted, keeping an account of the labor by them performed, of the value of it, and the expenses of their maintenance. The question of their final disposition will be reserved for future determination."

Two months later Congress made this official by passing a bill to confiscate all property used for insurrectionary purposes which provided, "That whenever any person claiming to be entitled to the services or labor of any other person, under the laws of any state, shall employ such persons in aiding or promoting any insurrection, or in resisting the laws of the United States, or shall permit or suffer him to be so employed, he shall forfeit all right to such service or labor, and the person whose labor or service is thus claimed shall be henceforth discharged therefrom; any law to the contrary notwithstanding."

There was a wide divergence of opinion among army commanders as to how this act should be interpreted. Many generals refused to be slave catchers. In Missouri General Henry Halleck ordered, "No fugitive slaves will be admitted within our lines or camps except when specially ordered by the general commanding." General Don Carlos Buell, commanding in Tennessee, wrote, "It has come to my knowledge that slaves sometimes make their way improperly into our lines; and in some instances they may be enticed there. . . . Several applications have been made to me by persons whose servants have been found in our camps; and in every instance that I know of the master has recovered his servant and taken him away." When several slaveowners appealed to General Joseph Hooker for the return of their property he commanded, "The brigadier-general commanding directs that they be permitted to visit all the camps of his command, in search of their property; and if found, that they be allowed to take possession of the same, without any interference whatever."

Many, if not most, of the regular army officers did not want to become involved in the slavery question, and some generals were frankly proslavery. Major General George B. McClellan, commanding the Army of the Potomac, may already have had an eye toward the 1864 Democratic Presidential nomination when he wrote Lincoln a long letter lecturing him on several aspects of how to run a war and opposing abolition. It read, in part, "Neither confiscation of propetry, political executions of persons, territorial organization of states, nor forcible abolition of slavery should be contemplated for a moment."

Some of the political generals took an opposite view. The most extreme was that of Major General John C. Fremont, who had been the unsuccessful Republican Presidential nominee in 1856. When he took command of the Department of Missouri in August, 1861, he declared martial law and issued an emancipation proclamation which decreed that "the property . . . of all persons in the State of Missouri who shall take up arms against the United States, or who shall be directly proven to have taken active part with their enemies in the field, is declared to be confiscated to the public use; and their slaves, if any they have, are hereby declared free men." Down in the Department of the South, Major General David Hunter proclaimed, "The persons in these states—Georgia, Florida and South Carolina—heretofore held as slaves, are therefore declared forever free."

Lincoln promptly countermanded both proclamations. He issued a proclamation of his own to counter Hunter's in which he said, "that neither General Hunter nor any other commander or person have been authorized by the Government of the United States to make proclamation declaring the slaves of any state free; and that the supposed proclamation now in question, whether genuine or false, is altogether void, so far as respects such declaration."

For the first year and a half of the war Lincoln still wisely trod the middle of the road, under constantly increasing pressure from both sides. The abolitionists were more vocal in condemning what they considered the President's weak-kneed policy on slavery. But Lincoln believed that the majority of the northern people were not in accord with the antislavery movement. To one visitor he said, "You possibly overestimate the number in the country who hold such views. But the position in which I am placed brings me into some knowledge of opinions in all parts of the country and of many different kinds of people; and it appears to me that the great masses of this country care comparatively little about the Negro, and are anxious only for military successes." He added, "When the hour comes for dealing with slavery, I trust that I will be willing to do my duty though it cost me my life."

The North was far from united in its views on slavery. The *New York Express* condemned antislavery agitation by shouting, "Down everywhere with the Negro! Down with him as the pest of parties and the curse of the country when mixed up with politics." *Harper's Weekly* sadly summarized popular feeling by editorializing, "There is very little moral mixture in the 'antislavery' feeling of this country. A great deal is abstract philanthropy; part is hatred of slaveholders; a great part is jealousy for white labor; very little is a consciousness of wrong done, and the wish to right it. How we hate those whom we have injured. I, too, 'tremble when I reflect that God is just.' "

The antislavery people pulled no punches in their castigation of the President. The American Antislavery Society in its annual report said that he was "under the delusion that soft words will salve the nation's sores," and analyzed his middle-of-the-road policy at length, saying that he was "a sort of bland respectable middleman, between a very modest Right and the most arrogant and exacting Wrong; a convenient hook whereon to hang appeals at once to a *moderate* antislavery feeling and to a timid conservatism practically proslavery, halfway assertions of human rights, and whole-way concessions to a wicked prejudice against dark-colored manhood, arguments against slavery extension, and apologies for continued complicity in slaveholding. He thinks slavery wrong, but opposes the immediate abolition of it; believes it ought to be kept out of the territories, but would admit it to the Union states; asserts the power of Congress to abolish it in the District of Columbia, but would have leave asked of the slaveholders for the exercise of that power; considers slave-

catching as a 'distasteful' business, but would enforce it by
congressional enactments, not only under but beyond the
Constitution's warrant for it; dislikes the slave trade, but
is not ready to forbid it between the states; affirms the
equality of white men and black in natural rights, but is
'not in favor of Negro citizenship'; in short, if we rightly
understand him, regards impartial justice as a most excellent thing, but as somewhat too fine and costly for every-
day wear."

Lincoln would not be rushed or bullied. Late in 1861 he
told one of the numerous committees of abolitionists that
haunted the White House, "It would do no good to go
ahead any faster than the country would follow. You know
the old Latin motto, *festina lente.* How do the Italians say
the same thing now?"

"They have improved on it, Mr. President. They say,
'Andante adagio, perchè ho premúra—'Go slow, because
I am in a hurry.' "

"That's it, exactly. I think Sumner and the rest of you
would upset our apple cart altogether, if you had your
way. We'll fetch 'em; just give us a little time. We didn't
go into the war to put down slavery, but to put the flag
back; and to act differently at this moment would, I have
no doubt, not only weaken our cause, but smack of bad
faith; for I never should have had votes enough to send
me here, if the people had supposed I should try to use my
power to upset slavery. Why, the first thing you would
see, would be a mutiny in the army. No! we must wait
until every other means has been exhausted. This thunder-
bolt will keep."

Lincoln's great concern for the timing of any action on
slavery was based on the probable reaction of the border
slave states. There was active support for the Union cause

in Maryland, Delaware, Missouri, Tennessee and Kentucky. But this support was for the restoration of the Union, *not* for the abolition of slavery. General emancipation was very different from the confiscation of slaves who were being used to support the southern war effort, and who might be returned to slavery after the war was over. Lincoln was sure that all sympathy for the Union cause in the border states would be alienated if the federal government moved against slavery as an institution.

In March, 1862, the President made the first tentative move toward emancipation in a message to Congress which proposed, "That the United States ought to co-operate with any state which may adopt gradual abolishment of slavery, giving to such state pecuniary aid, to be used by such state in its discretion to compensate for the inconvenience, public and private, produced by such a change of system."

The message continued to point out that his proposal was aimed principally at the border states. He wrote, "The point is not that *all* the states tolerating slavery would very soon, if at all, initiate emancipation; but that, while the offer is equally made to all, the more northern shall, by such initiation, make it certain to the more southern that in no event will the former ever join the latter in their proposed Confederacy. I say, 'initiation,' because in my judgment, gradual, and not sudden emancipation, is better for all." Congress passed the measure, although most of the representatives from the border states voted against it.

Four months later Lincoln called the border state congressmen to the White House to cajole and plead with them to urge its adoption in their own states. He said, "I intend no reproach or complaint when I assure you that, in my opinion, if you had all voted for the resolution . . .

of last March the war would now be substantially ended."
He pointed out that, if the war dragged on, slavery must
ultimately be extinguished by the friction of combat. He
reasoned, "How much better to thus save the money which
else we sink forever in the war! How much better to do it
while we can, lest the war ere long render us pecuniarily
unable to do it! How much better for you as seller, and
the nation as buyer, to sell out and buy out that without
which the war could never have been, than to sink both
the thing to be sold and the price of it in cutting one another's throats!" Most of the border state men reported
against Lincoln's proposal, and nothing came of the plan
to buy freedom for the slaves.

A few days after the White House conference with the
border states, Senator Sumner, who was constantly urging
emancipation on Lincoln, wrote to a friend in England:
"He is hard to move. He is honest but inexperienced. Thus
far he has been influenced by the border states. I urged him
on the Fourth of July to put forth an edict of emancipation,
telling him he could make the day more sacred and historic
than ever. He replied, 'I would do it if I were not afraid
that half the officers would fling down their arms and three
more states would rise.' He is plainly mistaken about the
officers, and I think also with regard to the states." The
Massachusetts senator also said that his severest trial was
"screwing Old Abe up to the sticking point," and, he
lamented, "How slow this child of freedom is being born."

Pressure for emancipation was coming from another
source. The American minister to Vienna, after visiting
Paris, London and Berlin, reported that European recognition of the Confederacy could be averted only by one of
three conditions—a smashing military victory for the
Union; the capture of a southern port and the release of

southern cotton to European factories; an announcement of a policy to emancipate the slaves. The minister at Madrid also wrote stressing this last point.

Lincoln sent to a friendly member of the British House of Commons a resolution which he might introduce in that body—perhaps the only occasion on which an American President has written proposed legislation for the English Parliament. It read:

"Whereas, while heretofore states and nations have tolerated slavery, recently, for the first [time] in the world, an attempt has been made to construct a new nation, upon the basis of, and with the primary and fundamental object to maintain, enlarge and perpetuate human slavery; therefore,

"*Resolved,* That no such embryo state should ever be recognized by, or admitted into, the family of Christian and civilized nations; and that all Christian and civilized men everywhere should, by all lawful means, resist to the utmost such recognition and admission."

It was the primary purpose of the Union foreign policy to prevent recognition of the Confederacy as a belligerent nation, rather than as a section of the United States in rebellion. Such recognition would have made it much easier for the South to secure war material from Europe, even without a military alliance. A paradoxical situation existed in Europe, particularly in England. Most of the government leaders favored the Confederacy because southern cotton was a basic material for their industry. But public opinion abroad was strongly antislavery—even on the part of the half million English millworkers who were unemployed for want of cotton.

Emancipation made some progress in the spring of 1862. In April Congress passed a bill liberating the slaves in the

District of Columbia, paying loyal owners $300 a head and appropriating $100,000 for their colonization. In June a bill was passed prohibiting slavery in the territories and freeing any slaves in these areas. This was followed by a bill which gave freedom to every Negro enrolled, drafted or volunteering for the armed forces.

The President kept harping on his two favorite themes— colonization and gradual, compensated emancipation. He induced Congress to recognize the Negro Republics of Haiti and Liberia. The State Department qualified the recognition by stipulating that a Negro would not be received as a foreign minister, at which Lincoln humphed to a Washington correspondent, "You can tell the President of Haiti that I shan't tear my shirt if he sends a nigger here."

On September 13, 1862, Lincoln made a lengthy statement on emancipation to a group of Chicago ministers who had come to urge the act on him, telling him it was the will of God. Lincoln first mildly questioned their authority to speak for the Almighty by saying, "I am approached with the most opposite opinions, and advice and that by religious men, who are equally certain that they represent the Divine will. I am sure that either the one or the other class is mistaken in that belief, and perhaps, in some respects, both. I hope it will not be irreverent for me to say that if it is probable that God would reveal His will to others, on a point so connected with my duty, it might be supposed He would reveal it directly to me; for, unless I am more deceived in myself than I often am, it is my earnest desire to know the will of Providence in this matter. And if I can learn what it is, I will do it!"

He then continued to advance several reasons why an act of emancipation was not practical at the moment.

"What good would a proclamation of emancipation from me do, especially as we are now situated? I do not want to issue a document that the whole world see must necessarily be inoperative, like the Pope's Bull against the Comet! Would my word free the slaves, when I cannot even enforce the Constitution in the rebel states? Is there a single court or magistrate, or individual that would be influenced by it there? And what reason is there to think it would have any greater effect upon the slaves than the late law of Congress, which I approved and which offers protection and freedom to the slaves of rebel masters who came within our lines? Yet I cannot learn that that law has caused a single slave to come over to us.

"And suppose they could be induced by a proclamation of freedom from me to throw themselves upon us, what should we do with them? How can we feed and care for such a multitude? General Butler wrote me a few days since that he was issuing more rations to the slaves who have rushed to him, than to all the white troops under his command. . . .

"Now, then, tell me, if you please, what possible result of good would follow the issuing of such a proclamation as you desire? Understand, I raise no objections against it on legal or constitutional grounds, for, as Commander-in-Chief of the Army and Navy, in time of war, I suppose I have a right to take any measure which may best subdue the enemy, nor do I urge objections of a moral nature, in view of possible consequences of insurrection and massacre at the South. I view this matter as a practical war measure, to be decided on according to the advantages or disadvantages it may offer to the suppression of the rebellion."

Lincoln admitted that "emancipation might help us in

Europe and convince them that we are incited by something more than ambition." He also agreed that "it would
weaken the rebels by drawing off their labor." But, he
added, "I am not so sure we could do much with the
blacks. If we were to arm them, I fear that in a few weeks
the arms would be in the hands of the rebels; and, indeed,
thus far, we have not had arms enough to equip our white
troops.

"I will mention another thing, though it meet only your
scorn and contempt. There are 50,000 bayonets in the
Union Army from the border slave states. It would be a
serious matter if, in consequence of a proclamation such
as you desire, they should go over to the rebels. I do not
think they all would—not so many, indeed, as a year ago,
or as six months ago—not so many today as yesterday.
Every day increases their Union feeling. They are also getting their pride enlisted, and want to beat the rebels."

He concluded by saying, "I have not decided against a
proclamation of liberty to the slaves, but hold the matter
under advisement. And I can assure you that the subject
is on my mind, by day and night, more than any other.
Whatever shall appear to be God's will I will do."

While Lincoln was making this lengthy dissertation to
the clergymen on why an emancipation proclamation was
not feasible, his announcement of the Emancipation Proclamation was laying in his desk—and had been for almost
two months.

Sometime in the late spring of 1862 Lincoln apparently
came to the conclusion that general emancipation was inevitable as a military and political maneuver. He tele-
graphed Leonard Swett, an old friend and fellow lawyer,
to come to Washington from Illinois. Closeted in the
Cabinet room, Lincoln gave Swett a letter from abolition-

ist William Lloyd Garrison saying that unless slavery was wiped out the basic purpose of the war would not be accomplished. After Swett had read this the President silently handed him a letter from a Kentucky senator saying that emancipation would throw the border states into the Confederacy. Next, Lincoln produced a letter from a Swiss statesman who warned that emancipation might be considered as an invitation for slave insurrections and invite European intervention on the basis that, throughout history, interference with the enemy's slaves had been considered as beyond the bounds of civilized warfare.

When Swett had read these and laid them aside Lincoln talked for an hour on all aspects of emancipation—turning the subject inside out and upside down. According to Swett, the President did not seem to be trying to convince him of anything; nor did he ask Swett's opinion. He was merely using his old friend as a sounding board to explore his own mind. After the lecture was over Swett got back on the cars for his two-day trip home.

On July 22, 1862, Lincoln called a meeting of his Cabinet and laid before them what is now called the Preliminary Emancipation Proclamation. Painter Frank Carpenter, who accurately recorded his conversations with the President while he was painting his portrait, left this account of the meeting and of the subsequent issuance of the preliminary proclamation as it was given to him by Lincoln:

"Things had gone on from bad to worse, until I felt that we had reached the end of our rope on the plan of operations we had been pursuing; that we had about played our last card, and must change our tactics, or lose the game. I now determined upon the adoption of the emancipation policy, and without consultation with or the knowledge of the Cabinet, I prepared the original draft of the proclamation, and after much anxious thought, called a Cabinet meeting upon the subject. I said to the Cabinet that I had resolved upon this step, and had not called them together to ask their advice, but to lay the subject matter of a proclamation before them, suggestions as to which would be in order, after they had heard it read. Secretary [of the Treasury] Chase wished the language stronger in reference to the arming of the blacks. Mr. Blair [Postmaster General] deprecated the policy, on the ground that it would cost the administration the fall elections.

"Nothing, however, was offered that I had not already fully anticipated and settled in my own mind, until Secretary [of State] Seward spoke. He said in substance, 'Mr. President, I approve of the proclamation, but I question the expediency of its issue at this juncture. The depression of the public mind, consequent upon our repeated reverses, is so great that I fear the effect of so important a step. It may be viewed as the last measure of an exhausted government, a cry for help; the government stretching forth its hands to Ethiopia, instead of Ethiopia stretching forth her hands to the government.' His idea was that it would be considered our last *shriek*, on the retreat. 'Now,' continued Mr. Seward, 'while I approve the measure, I suggest, sir, that you postpone its issue, until you can give it to the country supported by military success, instead of issuing it, as would be the case now, upon the greatest disasters of the war.' The wisdom of the view of the Secretary of State struck me with very great force. It was an aspect of the case that, in all my thought upon the subject, I had entirely overlooked.

"The result was that I put the draft of the proclamation

aside. . . . From time to time I added or changed a line, touching it up here and there, anxiously awaiting the progress of events. Well, the next news we had was of Pope's disaster, at Bull Run. Things looked darker than ever. Finally, came the week of the battle of Antietam. I determined to wait no longer. The news came, I think, on Wednesday, that the advantage was on our side. I was then staying at the Soldier's Home [three miles out of Washington]. Here I finished writing the second draft of the preliminary proclamation, came up on Saturday, called the Cabinet together to hear it, and it was published the following Monday."

During the summer Lincoln spent much time in the telegraph office, receiving at first hand the bad news from the fighting front. Between clickings of the keys he made the minor changes to which he referred in his conversation with Carpenter. Then, on September 22, after Lee's attempted invasion of Maryland had failed with the bloody fighting at Antietam, he called another Cabinet meeting. Treasury Secretary Salmon Chase and Secretary of the Navy Gideon Welles recorded the President's comments at this one. After reminding them of the proclamation which he had presented to them two months earlier, the President continued:

"I have thought all along that the time for acting on it might probably come. I think the time has come now. I wish it was a better time. I wish that we were in a better condition. The action of the army against the rebels has not been quite what I should have best liked. But they have been driven out of Maryland, and Pennsylvania is no longer in danger of invasion. When the rebel army was at Frederick, I determined, as soon as it should be driven out of Maryland, to issue a proclamation of emancipation, such as I thought most likely to be useful. I said nothing to anyone; but I made the promise to myself and to my Maker. The rebel army is now driven out, and I am going to fulfill that promise.

"I have got you together to hear what I have written down. I do not wish your advice about the main matter; for that I have determined for myself. This I say without intending anything but respect for any one of you. But I already know the views of each on this question. They have been heretofore expressed, and I have considered them as thoroughly and carefully as I can. What I have written is that which my reflections have determined me to say. If there is anything in the expressions I use, or in any other minor matter, which any one of you thinks had best be changed, I shall be glad to receive the suggestions.

"One other observation I will make. I know very well that many others might, in this matter as in others, do better than I can; and if I was satisfied that the public confidence was more fully possessed by any one of them than by me, and knew of any constitutional way in which he could be put in my place, he should have it. I would gladly yield it to him. But though I believe that I have not so much of the confidence of the people as I had, some time since, I do not know that, all things considered, any person has more; and, however this may be, there is no way in which I can have any other man put where I am. I am here. I must do the best I can, and bear the responsibility of taking the course which I feel I ought to take."

In the opening paragraphs of the Preliminary Emancipation Proclamation Lincoln set forth that the primary purpose of the war was to restore "the constitutional relation between the United States and each of the states and the people thereof." He said that it was his purpose, at the next meeting of Congress, "to again recommend the adoption of practical measures tendering pecuniary aid" to bring about the gradual emancipation in slave states which were not in rebellion. He added that efforts toward colonization would be continued. Then came the key paragraph:

"That on the first day of January, in the year of our Lord one thousand eight hundred and sixty-three, all Persons held as Slaves within any State or designated part of a State, the people whereof shall then be in Rebellion against the United States, shall be then thenceforward, and forever Free; and the Executive Government of the United States, including the Military and Naval authority thereof, will recognize and maintain the Freedom of such persons, and will do no act or acts to repress such persons, or any of them, in any efforts they may make for their actual Freedom."

There were additional paragraphs which created a new Article of War forbidding the military to return fugitive slaves; providing that no fugitive slave should be returned from a free state unless his owner took an oath that he had not born arms against the United States nor given aid or comfort to rebels; and promising the Executive would recommend that, upon the termination of the war, all loyal slaveholders would be compensated for the loss of slaves. But the great words were two in the key paragraph: forever free.

The Preliminary Emancipation Proclamation was issued on September 24, 1862. Lincoln said that "public sentiment" would not have stood for it six months before. As usual, he told one of his little parables, "A man watches his pear tree day after day, impatient for the ripening of the fruit. Let him attempt to *force* the process and he may spoil both fruit and tree. But let him patiently *wait*, and the ripe pear at length falls into his lap." When a crowd gathered at the White House the President told them from the balcony, "What I did, I did after a very full delibera-ation. . . . I can only trust in God I have made no mistake, I shall make no attempt on this occasion to sustain what I have done or said by any comment. It is now for the coun-try and the world to pass judgment, and, maybe, take action upon it."

The President's Proclamation received what is called in theatrical parlance "mixed notices." Sixteen free state gov-ernors were about to meet in Pennsylvania to put pressure on Lincoln. The Proclamation took the wind out of their sails and they adopted a resolution endorsing the Presi-dent's new policy. Although Lincoln said that he "never thought of the governors" in connection with his action, their resolution may have lessened the extent of the Repub-lican losses in the November elections.

General McClellan wrote his wife that he was thinking of resigning his commission in protest against the Procla-mation. Garrison wrote that he "was not so jubilant" be-cause the Proclamation did not free all the slaves. The *New York Express* said that the Proclamation would be bad for business. The *New York World* said that the South would now fight harder. The *New York Journal of Commerce* condemned Lincoln for making law by proclamation.

A wave of fury swept the South, which saw the Procla-mation as outside the pale of the rules of war and a deliberate incitement to slaves to kill, rape and burn. Con-federate General G. T. Beauregard wired Richmond to propose executing abolitionist prisoners after January 1, adding: "It is high time to proclaim the black flag after that period. Let the execution be by garrote." Jefferson Davis told the Confederate Congress that the Proclamation could have, "but one of three possible consequences—the extermination of the slaves, the exile of the whole white population of the Confederacy, or absolute and total separation of these states from the United States." He added, "Our own detestation of those who have attempted the most execrable measures recorded in the history of guilty man is tempered by profound contempt for the impotent rage which it discloses," and then asked congressional permission to turn over captured Union officers to the several states for punishment as "criminals engaged in inciting servile insurrection."

In England the Proclamation was generally condemned by press and government. The London *Times* found it "a very sad document." The *Standard* called it "the makeshift of a pettifogging lawyer." In Parliament one member labeled it "a hideous outburst of weak but demoniacal spite," another, "one of the most devilish acts of fiendish malignity which the wickedness of man could ever have conceived." Henry Adams wrote from England that London "was altogether beside itself on one point; it created a nightmare of its own and gave it the shape of Abraham Lincoln." But while England's statesmen fumed, Lincoln's action had the widespread support of British public opinion. The chance for English recognition of the Confederacy faded.

Northern public opinion was expressed at the polls six weeks after the Preliminary Proclamation was issued. In almost all states the Republican majority fell off drastically, and New York, New Jersey, Pennsylvania, Ohio, Indiana and Illinois went Democratic. The President's party kept control of Congress by but a slim margin, as Democratic congressional strength rose from forty-four to seventy-five. Dissatisfaction with the cost of the war and the military situation had much to do with this, as did the absence from the polls of several hundred thousand Republicans who were in the armed services. But there was some truth in the comment of the *New York Tribune* that the voters were serving notice on Lincoln that the war was for the restoration of the Union and not for "the bloody extermination of slavery."

There was much favorable newspaper comment on the Proclamation, and many prominent individuals endorsed it. Still, Lincoln, in a letter to Vice President Hannibal Hamlin marked "Strictly Private," remarked rather ruefully, "The time for its effect southward has not come; but northward the effect should be instantaneous. It is six days old, and while commendation in newspapers and by distinguished individuals is all that a vain man could wish, the stocks have declined, and troops come forward more slowly than ever. This, looked soberly in the face, is not very satisfactory."

In December, 1862, a month before the actual Emancipation Proclamation was to be issued, Lincoln devoted his Second Annual Message to Congress to his favorite plan of compensated emancipation, preferably associated with colonization, by proposing an amendment to the Constitution to make the plan effective. His plan was now more detailed. It proposed to compensate states which emancipated slaves by January 1, 1900, with interest-bearing United States bonds, to be delivered in installments as the slaves were freed. He presented his plan to Congress with long and somewhat involved mathematical calculations to prove that it would be cheaper in the long run to pay for the slaves than to pay for the war. Then he veered to attack the contention that four million freed slaves would "injure and displace white labor and white laborers." He insisted that this view was unfounded, saying, "Is it true, then, that colored people can displace any more white labor by being free, than by remaining slaves? If they stay in their old places, they jostle no white laborers; if they leave their old places, they leave them open to white laborers. Logically, there is neither more nor less of it.

"Emancipation, even without deportation, would probably enhance the wages of white labor, and very surely would not reduce them. Thus, the customary amount of labor would still have to be performed; the freed people would surely not do more than their old proportion of it and, very probably, for a time would do less, leaving an increased part to white laborers, bringing their labor into greater demand, and consequently enhancing the wages of it. With deportation, even to a limited extent, enhanced wages to white labor is mathematically certain. . . .

"But it is dreaded that the freed people will swarm forth and cover the whole land! Are they not already in the land? Will liberation make them any more numerous? Why should emancipation South, send the freed people North? People of any color seldom run, unless there be something to run from. Heretofore, colored people, to some extent, have fled North from bondage, and now, perhaps, from both bondage and destitution. But if gradual emancipation and deportation be adopted, they will have neither to flee from. Their old masters will give them wages at least until new laborers can be procured; and the freed men, in turn, will gladly give their labor for the wages, till new homes can be found for them, in congenial climes, and with people of their own blood and race. This proposition can be trusted on the mutual interests involved. And, in any event, cannot the North decide for itself, whether to receive them?"

The President concluded his long address on an inspiring note, "In *giving* freedom to the *slave,* we *assure* freedom to the *free*—honorable alike in what we give and what we preserve. We shall nobly save, or meanly lose, the last, best hope of earth. Other means may succeed; this could not fail. The way is plain, peaceful, generous, just— a way which, if followed, the world would forever applaud, and God must forever bless."

As January 1, 1863, approached there was much speculation as to whether Lincoln would actually issue the Proclamation he had promised in September. Even in the Beecher family opinion was divided. Harriet Breecher Stowe was sure that he would and wrote Senator Sumner, "Please do not forget to express to the President my suggestion that he recommend solemn religious services on that day." Henry Ward Beecher thought that he would not, saying, "It is far easier to slide down the banisters than to go up the stairs."

On the Sunday before New Year's Day Dr. Byron Sunderland, chaplain of the Senate, preached an antislavery sermon and then called on the President. He frankly asked Lincoln, "Mr. President, they say you are not going to keep your promise to give us the Emancipation Proclamation; that it is your intention to withdraw it."

"Well, Doctor," said the President, "you know Peter was going to do it, but when the time came he did not."

"Mr. President, I have been studying Peter," continued Sunderland. "He did not deny his Master until after his Master rebuked him in the presence of the enemy. You have a master, too, Mr. Lincoln, the American people. Don't deny your master till he has rebuked you before all the world."

Lincoln then turned serious and, according to Dr. Sunderland, said, "Doctor, if it had been left to you and me, there would have been no war. If it had been left to you and me, there would have been no cause for this war; but it was not left to us. God has allowed men to make slaves of their fellows. He permits this war. He has before Him a strange spectacle. We, on our side, are praying Him to give us victory, because we believe we are right; but those on the other side pray Him, too, for victory, believing they are right. What must He think of us? And what is coming from the struggle? What will be the effect of it all on the whites and on the Negroes?"

Returning to his jocular tone the President then said, "As for the Negroes, Doctor, and what is going to become of them: I told Ben Wade the other day that it made me think of a story I read in one of my first books, *Aesop's Fables*. It was an old edition, and had curious rough wood-cuts, one of which showed four white men scrubbing a Negro in a potash kettle filled with cold water. The text explained that the men thought that by scrubbing the Negro they might make him white. Just about the time they thought they were succeeding, he took cold and died. Now, I am afraid that by the time we get through this war the Negro will catch cold and die."

There was never any need for concern as to whether Lincoln would fulfill his announced intention to issue the Proclamation. Since his soul-searching session with Swett six months before, he had accepted the step as inevitable and had never indicated any intention to turn from it. As the day neared he told a White House visitor, "I have studied that matter well; my mind is made up. . . . *It must be done. I am driven to it.* There is no other way out of our troubles. But although my duty is plain, it is in some respects painful, and I trust the people will understand that I act not in anger but in expectation of a greater good."

Abraham Lincoln distributed copies of the Emancipation Proclamation to the Cabinet on December 30. Some minor changes were suggested, and Secretary Chase submitted a new final paragraph which Lincoln accepted. Chase also thought that the slaves in the thirteen parishes in Louisiana, around New Orleans, and the counties in Virginia around Norfolk should not be excepted from emancipation. Seward supported him, as did Blair, who reasoned that posterity would wonder why this was done.

Lincoln pointed out that the area in question had been conquered by the Union and had established governments which were returning representatives to the northern Congress. These sections were therefore in the same category as the slave states which were not in rebellion and which were also excepted in the Proclamation. Chase argued that Congress might not seat the southern representatives, fearing an increase in proslavery sentiment in the House. Lincoln replied with some heat, "I am to be bullied by Congress, am I? If I do I'll be durned." There was no further argument nor additional changes in the Proclamation.

On New Year's Day the President held the usual White House reception in the morning, shaking hands for hours with hundreds of visitors. That afternoon Secretary Seward and his son walked over to the White House with the original of the document, which had been left at the State Department to be engrossed. It needed only the President's signature. Lincoln dipped his pen and then paused, pen in air. "I never in my life," he said, "felt more certain that I was doing right, than I do in signing this paper. But I have been receiving calls and shaking hands since nine o'clock this morning, till my arm is stiff and numb. Now this signature is one that will be closely examined, and if they find my hand trembled they will say, 'he had some compunctions.' But anyway, it is going to be done."

He then slowly and carefully signed "Abraham Lincoln" at the bottom of the Emancipation Proclamation. The signature was, perhaps, a trifle tremulous, but it was bold and clear. That evening the telegraph carried to the nation and the world the text of the most momentous American document since the Constitution. As a piece of prose it was not inspired—was, in fact, dry and formal and rather dull. But it was the most exciting and controversial news that the nation had heard in many a day. It read:

BY THE PRESIDENT OF THE UNITED STATES OF AMERICA:

A Proclamation.

Whereas, on the twenty-second day of September, in the year of our Lord one thousand eight hundred and sixty-two, a proclamation was issued by the President of the United States, containing, among other things, the following, to wit:

That on the first day of January, in the year of our Lord one thousand eight hundred and sixty-three, all persons held as slaves within any State or designated part of a State, the people whereof shall then be in rebellion against the United States, shall be then, thenceforward, and forever, free; and the Executive government of the United States, including the military and naval authority thereof, will recognize and maintain the freedom of such persons, and will do no act or acts to repress such persons, or any of them, in any efforts they may make for their actual freedom.

That the Executive will, on the first day of January aforesaid, by proclamation, designate the States and parts of States, if any, in which the people thereof, respectively, shall then be in rebellion against the United States; and the fact that any State, or the people thereof, shall on that day be in good faith represented in the Congress of the United States, by members chosen thereto at elections wherein a majority of the qualified voters of such State shall have participated, shall, in the absence of strong countervailing testimony, be deemed conclusive evidence that such State, and the people thereof, are not then in rebellion against the United States.

Now, therefore I, Abraham Lincoln, President of the United States, by virtue of the power in me vested as commander-in-chief of the army and navy of the United States in time of actual armed rebellion against the authority and government of the United States, and as a fit and necessary war measure for suppressing said rebellion, do, on this first day of January, in the year of our Lord one thousand eight hundred and sixty-three, and in accordance with my purpose so to do, publicly proclaimed for the full period of one hundred days from the first day above mentioned, order and designate as the States and parts of States wherein the people thereof, respectively, are this day in rebellion against the United States, the following, to wit:

Arkansas, Texas, Louisiana (except the Parishes of St. Bernard, Plaquemines, Jefferson, St. John, St. Charles, St. James, Ascension, Assumption, Terre Bonne, Lafourche, St. Mary, St. Martin, and Orleans, including the city of New Orleans), Mississippi, Alabama, Florida, Georgia, South Carolina, North Carolina, and Virginia (except the forty-eight counties designated as West Virginia, and also the counties of Berkeley, Accomac, Northhampton, Elizabeth City, York, Princess Anne and Norfolk, including the cities of Norfolk and Portsmouth), and which excepted parts are for the present left precisely as if this proclamation were not issued.

And by the virtue of the power and for the purpose aforesaid, I do order and declare that all persons held as slaves within said designated States, and parts of States are and henceforward shall be free; and that the Executive government of the United States, including the military and naval authorities thereof, will recognize and maintain the freedom of said persons.

And I here enjoin upon the people so declared to be free to abstain from all violence, unless in necessary self-defence; and

I recommend to them that, in all cases when allowed, they labor faithfully for reasonable wages.

And I further declare and make known that such persons of suitable condition, will be received into the armed service of the United States, to garrison forts, positions, stations, and other places, and to man vessels of all sorts in said service.

And upon this act, sincerely believed to be an act of justice warranted by the Constitution upon military necessity, I invoke the considerate judgment of mankind and the gracious favor of Almighty God.

In witness whereof, I have herunto set my hand and caused the seal of the United States to be affixed.

(SEAL) Done at the city of Washington this first day of January, in the year of our Lord one thousand eight hundred and sixty-three, and of the independence of the United States of America the eighty-seventh.

Abraham Lincoln

The deed was done. The slaves were free—or at least *some* slaves were *proclaimed* free. The death knell of the evil "peculiar institution" had sounded. Up in Massachusetts Henry Wadsworth Longfellow wrote in his diary before he retired on that New Year's Day, "A great day. The President's Proclamation for Emancipation of slaves in the rebel states goes into effect. A beautiful day, full of sunshine, ending in a tranquil moonlight night. May it be symbolical."

Freedom and Aftermath

During the first two years of the war several steps had been taken on the road to freedom. Early in the conflict Congress had declared free slaves who were used by the enemy for military work. Negroes flocked to the Union lines, and Congress ruled that officers who returned them to their owners would be dismissed from the service. The federal government had purchased and freed the slaves of the District of Columbia. Slavery was forever outlawed in the territories. Later, all slaves who made their way into Union camps were declared free if they were owned by slaveholders who were aiding the enemy. The President was authorized to receive into the military service "persons of African descent," and if such slaves had wives, children or enslaved parents who were owned by somebody who was aiding the enemy, they too were free. All fugitive slave laws had been repealed.

All of this liberated something over a million slaves—

almost a third of the total. Then the Emancipation Proclamation *announced* that all slaves in certain areas were forever free. But in terms of actually freeing slaves the Proclamation did nothing. Slaves in the enemy country to which the Proclamation was limited could no more be freed by proclaiming their freedom than a military victory could be won by declaring it. Yet in another sense, the Proclamation did everything. It stirred the red blood in black bodies with a magical, a mystical, hope. One hundred and thirty thousand Negroes who bore arms for the Union now had something personal to fight for.

Perhaps the clearest, coldest, unemotional analysis of the document came from the British Foreign Minister in a letter to England's ambassador in Washington. He wrote, "The Proclamation *professes* to emancipate all slaves in places where the United States authorities cannot exercise any jurisdiction nor make emancipation a reality; but it does not *decree* emancipation of slaves in any states or parts of states occupied by federal troops. . . . There seems to be no declaration of a principle adverse to slavery in this proclamation. It is a measure of war of a very questionable kind."

But though Lord Russell might grumble about the Proclamation not being in good taste by British standards, the people who could vote Lord Russell's party out of office held a different view. From London Henry Adams wrote, "The Emancipation Proclamation has done more for us here than all our former victories and all our diplomacy. It is creating an almost convulsive reaction in our favor all over this country."

At home, opinion continued mixed, as it had after the Preliminary Proclamation. Lincoln spent much time trying to justify his act. A year after the fact he was still writing such letters as this: "I am naturally antislavery. If slavery is not wrong, nothing is wrong. I cannot remember when I did not so think and feel, and yet I have never understood that the Presidency conferred upon me an unrestricted right to act officially upon this judgment and feeling. . . . And I aver that, to this day, I have done no official act in mere deference to my abstract judgment and feeling on slavery.

"I did understand, however, that my oath to preserve the Constitution to the best of my ability, imposed upon me the duty of preserving by every indispensable means, that government—that nation—of which that Constitution was the organic Law.

"Was it possible to lose the nation and yet preserve the Constitution?

"By general law, life and limb must be protected; yet often a limb must be amputated to save a life; but a life is never wisely given to save a limb. I felt that measures, otherwise unconstitutional, might become lawful, by becoming indispensable to the Constitution through the preservation of the nation. Right or wrong, I assumed this ground, and now avow it. I could not feel that, to the best of my ability, I have even tried to preserve the Constitution, if, to save slavery, or any minor matter, I should permit the wreck of government, country, and Constitution, altogether. . . .

"More than a year of trial now shows no loss by it in our foreign relations, none in our home popular sentiment, none in our white military force, no loss by it anyhow, or anywhere. On the contrary, it shows a gain of quite a hundred and thirty thousand soldiers, seamen, and laborers."

In the summer of 1863 a group of anti-emancipation Unionists held a mass meeting in Chicago and asked Lincoln to attend. The President declined, but wrote them a long letter to justify his position, in which he said, in part, "You are dissatified with me about the Negro. Quite likely there is a difference of opinion between you and myself upon that subject. I certainly wish that all men could be free, while you, I suppose, do not. Yet I have neither adopted nor proposed any measure which is not consistent with your view, provided you are for the Union. . . .

"You dislike the Emanciaption Proclamation, and perhaps would have it retracted. You say it is unconstitutional. I think differently. I think that the Constitution invests its Commander-in-Chief with the law of war in time of war. The most that can be said, if so much, is that the slaves are property. Is there, has there ever been, any question that by the law of war, property both of enemies and friends may be taken when needed? And is it not needed whenever taking it helps us or hurts the enemy? Armies, the world over, destroy enemies' property when they cannot use it; and even destroy their own to keep it from the enemy. Civilized belligerents do all in their power to help themselves or hurt the enemy, except a few things regarded as barbarous or cruel. . . .

"You say that you will not fight to free Negroes. Some of them seem to be willing to fight for you—but no matter. Fight you, then, exclusively to save the Union. I issued the Proclamation on purpose to aid you in saving the Union. Whenever you shall have conquered all resistance to the Union, if I shall urge you to continue fighting, it will be an apt time then for you to declare that you will not fight to free Negroes. I thought that in your struggle for the Union, to whatever extent the Negroes should cease helping the enemy, to that extent it weakened the enemy in his resistance to you. Do you think differently? I thought whatever Negroes can be got to do as soldiers, leaves just so much less for white soldiers to do in saving the Union. Does it appear otherwise to you? But Negroes, like other people, act upon motives. Why should they do anything for us if we will do nothing for them? If they stake their lives for us they must be prompted by the strongest motive, even the promise of freedom. And the promise being made must be kept."

In his annual message to Congress in December, 1863, almost a year after the Proclamation had been issued, Lincoln set at rest all talk that it would be revoked by stating, "While I remain in my present position I shall not attempt to retract or modify the Emancipation Proclamation; nor shall I return to slavery any person who is free by the terms of that Proclamation; or by any of the acts of Congress." He again advocated his favorite method of gradual, compensated emancipation—"while I do not repeat in detail what I have heretofore so earnestly urged upon this subject, my general views and feelings remain unchanged."

Lincoln never tried to justify the Proclamation on moral grounds, and he admittedly was not easy in his mind about its legal validity. Although he thought that his action was morally right, he attributed it solely to necessity as a military and diplomatic measure. It encouraged Negro enlistments in the Union forces. It could be expected to have at least a strong psychological effect on the southern Negroes who were building railroads and fortifications, driving wagons and growing food for the southern forces. It encouraged them to try to escape, if not to revolt; and without their labor the Confederacy would quickly collapse. So it was right and it was necessary—but was it legal? Most experts in both constitutional and international law say no.

Certainly Lincoln's claim that he was justified in depriving the enemy of any property that would enhance their capacity for making war was valid. The catch was in the words "are and henceforward shall be free." Neither law nor the accepted rules of war gave the Commander-in-Chief the right *permanently* to confiscate personal property. Under international law such property should be returned, or claims for it judged, after the war was over. The position of the United States government on this point had been made clear at the end of the War of 1812. The English invaders had freed many American slaves and carried them to England or the West Indies. The United States demanded payment for this property, and England, although strongly antislavery, agreed to pay. Russia acted as arbiter to set the amount at three million dollars.

If one took the position that international law did not apply to a rebellion or civil war, then Lincoln could justify confiscation of property only as a punishment for treason; and this could be done legally only after the treasonable parties had been convicted by a jury trial.

There were only two ways in which the freeing of slaves would be unquestionably legal. One was by emancipation through acts of each slave state individually. The other was by a constitutional amendment.

Such an amendment, providing that "slavery is hereby forever prohibited in all the states of the Union and in all territories now owned, or which may hereafter be acquired," was introduced in the House of Representatives in December, 1863. A similar resolution was proposed in the Senate. For six months it was a subject of bitter debate, largely along party rather than sectional lines. Some border state Democrats were for it; most free state Democrats were against it. When it finally came to a vote it failed to get the necessary two-thirds majority, and despite the Emancipation Proclamation, slavery remained the law of the land.

In mid-1864 both the President and the Republican party took a strong stand on general emancipation. The convention which nominated Lincoln for a second term also adopted a plank which said that "slavery was the cause and now constitutes the strength of the rebellion . . . justice and the national safety demands its utter and complete extirpation from the soil of the republic. . . . We are in favor, furthermore of such an amendment to the Constitution . . . as shall terminate and forever prohibit the existence of slavery within the limits or the jurisdiction of the United States."

In July, 1864, Lincoln went on record as demanding abolition of slavery as a condition of peace. Horace Greeley —always something of a "busybody"—received a letter from a man named Jewett saying that there were three accredited Confederate peace commissioners in Canada and asking Greeley to arrange for them to see Lincoln. When Greeley contacted Lincoln the President wrote him, "If you can find any person, anywhere, professing to have any proposition of Jefferson Davis in writing, for peace, embracing the restoration of the Union and abandonment of slavery, whatever else it embraces, say to him he may come to me with you."

Greeley went to Niagara Falls, New York, and talked to Jewett, where he learned that the supposed commissioners had no authority from Richmond, but claimed they could get it if they had a statement from Lincoln as to peace terms. Lincoln promptly sent his secretary, John Hay, to Canada with a letter in his own hand which read:

"To whom it may concern: Any proposition which embraces the restoration of peace, the integrity of the whole Union, and the abandonment of slavery, and which comes

by and with an authority that can control the armies now at war against the United States, will be received and considered by the executive government of the United States, and will be met by liberal terms on other substantial and collateral points, and the bearer or bearers thereof shall have safe conduct both ways."

The so-called Confederate commissioners wrote a long letter to Greeley which expressed indignation at Lincoln's demands, which, they said, were "a rude withdrawal of a courteous overture of negotiations." The publication of this letter aroused fresh attacks on Lincoln as an abolitionist. The *New York Herald* said that northern people were not interested in freeing the slaves. "What they want is the Union. The people have never before been officially told that the abolition of slavery will be insisted on as a *ne plus ultra* in the terms of peace, and are by no means pleased with the idea."

It is possible that this somewhat melodramatic incident on the Canadian border was inspired by Greeley or Jewett to provide seeming substance for the Democrat claim that Lincoln would not negotiate for peace. If so, it misfired—and provided another step on the long road to freedom by putting Lincoln on record that the "abandonment of slavery" was necessary for peace.

The 1864 elections, in addition to returning Lincoln to the White House, increased antislavery strength in Congress sufficiently to assure the passage of an antislavery amendment by the next Congress—but this would not meet, unless a special session was called, until the fall of 1865. But the President was now in a hurry to secure constitutional confirmation of his Proclamation and extend it to all slaves. In his December message he reminded the lame-duck Congress, "A proposed amendment of the Constitution, abolishing slavery throughout the United States, passed the Senate, but failed for lack of the requisite two-thirds vote in the House of Representatives." He would not question "the wisdom or patriotism of those who stood in opposition," while venturing to recommend reconsideration and passage of the measure at the present session. "Of course the abstract question is not changed, but an intervening election shows, almost certainly, that the next Congress will pass the measure if this does not. Hence there is only a question of time as to when the proposed amendment will go to the states for their action. And as it is to so go, at all events, may we not agree that the sooner the better?" He suggested to congressmen that their judgment might be affected by "the voice of the people," for the first time endorsing a party whose platform declared for the abolition of slavery.

A new amendment was introduced in both Houses. Numbered as Article XIII of the Constitution, it read,

"Section 1. Neither slavery nor involuntary servitude, except as a punishment for a crime whereof the party shall have been duly convicted, shall exist within the United States, or any place subject to their jurisdiction.

"Section 2. Congress shall have power to enforce this article by appropriate legislation."

The Thirteenth Amendment was sure of passage by the Senate. The vote in the House was another matter. Here success was very doubtful; and Lincoln the politician went to work behind the scenes to gather the few critical votes to provide the necessary two-thirds majority. He had already taken one step toward this goal by instigating the admission of Nevada to the Union, adding her votes to the antislavery block.

Lincoln is today remembered largely as a great humanitarian—is recalled by such emotional utterances as the Gettysburg Address and Second Inaugural Address which are emblazoned upon his monument. Most popular biographers ignore or minimize his role as a practical politician. But he was the shrewdest politician who had occupied the White House to that time. He kept the reigns of patronage tightly grasped in his own hands and used jobs and favors freely to get support when he needed it. He believed that he needed two votes to assure a two-thirds majority in the House. Representative John Alley of Massachusetts recorded how he got them:

"Two members of the House were sent for, and Mr. Lincoln said that those two votes must be procured. When asked, 'How?' he remarked: 'I am President of the United States, clothed with great power. The abolition of slavery by constitutional provision settles the fate, for all coming time, not only of the millions now in bondage, but of unborn millions to come—a measure of such importance that *those two votes must be procured.* I leave it to you to determine how it shall be done; but remember that I am President of the United States, clothed with immense power, and I expect you to procure those votes.' These gentlemen understood the significance of the remark. The votes were procured."

There is no record of what kind of a deal Lincoln made to get the votes or how he proposed to use his "immense power." One assumption is that the congressmen to whom he was talking were favorable to the bill and were given *carte blanche* on patronage promises to convert two of their colleagues. Another view is that Lincoln's visitors were opposed to abolition but had friends or relatives in prison and that Lincoln traded pardons for their votes.

The President's patient cultivation of the border state

men paid off in securing the passage of the Thirteenth Amendment. The necessary majority could not be obtained without their support, and only Lincoln's carefully developed friendships and his long record as a moderate rather than a radical abolitionist could secure that support. Congressman James Rollins was one of the largest slaveholders in Missouri. Lincoln called him to the White House, and after reminding him that they were "both old Whigs" from long before the war, he made a personal plea for Rollins to use his influence with Missouri and Kentucky representatives to support the amendment, saying, "The passage of this amendment will clinch the whole subject. It will bring the war, I have no doubt, rapidly to a close." When, during the congressional debate on the national amendment, Missouri amended its constitution to abolish slavery in the state, Rollins took the floor in the House to make an impassioned speech, saying, "I am no longer the owner of a slave, and I thank God for it. . . . To restore peace and preserve this Union, if I had owned a thousand slaves, they would most cheerfully have been given up. I say with all my heart, let them go, but let them not go without a sense of feeling and a proper regard on my part for the future of themselves and their offspring."

The bitter debate on the amendment continued right down to the wire on January 31, 1865. Only Democrats spoke—the Republicans were there to vote, not to argue. McAllister of Pennsylvania said that he was going to cast his vote "against the cornerstone of the southern confederacy." Coffroth of Pennsylvania said that if by his vote for the measure, "I dig my political grave, I will descend into it without a murmur." But Miller of Pennsylvania held an opposing view. The amendment, he said was a "broad farce," and added, "Abolish slavery, and no man . . .

has pretended to show what we are to do with the freedmen, except that as good Christians, it will become our duty to feed and clothe them. The true philanthropists and taxpayers of the country are equally interested in knowing what is to be done with the elephant when we get him."

As the day waned, the floor and gallery of the House became so thronged that standing room was at a premium. Most of the members of the Senate had come over to line the walls, plus several Cabinet members and five Supreme Court justices. In that more mannerly day, when "a throng of richly dressed ladies" entered the gallery the members of the press gave them their seats.

When the roll call finally started the members who came first alphabetically were, by coincidence, all Republicans—Alley, Allison, Ames, Anderson, etc. The crowd was silent until James English, a Connecticut Democrat, shouted "Aye." Then there was a wild burst of applause. With each additional Democrat "Aye," the tumult mounted. The busy pencils of the press ticked off the votes. Down to the very end nothing was certain. A two-thirds majority was 122 votes. When the roll call was over there were 119 "Yeas." But there were only 56 "Nays"—8 members, all Democrats, had failed to vote. The Thirteenth Amendment had passed, but a shift of only three votes would have killed it. It was a Republican triumph which, in a sense, was made possible by the 8 Democrats who had abstained from voting.

At long last slavery was abolished—or would be on December 18, 1865, when the Thirteenth Amendment was formally proclaimed in effect after its ratification by twenty-seven states. Illinois ratified the day after the House vote, and Lincoln commented, "This ends the job. I feel proud that Illinois is a little ahead." That night, as he addressed a torchlit crowd from the balcony of the White House, the President admitted his doubts as to the legality of the Emancipation Proclamation. He said that he thought that all would bear him witness that he had never shrunk from doing all that he could to eradicate slavery, by issuing an Emancipation Proclamation, but the Proclamation fell far short of what the amendment would do when fully consummated. And, he added, "A question might be raised whether the Proclamation was legally valid. It might be added that it aided only those who did not give themselves up; or that it would have no effect upon the children of the slaves born hereafter; in fact, it could be urged that it did not meet the evil. But this amendment is a king's cure for all evils. It winds the whole thing up."

While state legislatures were busily ratifying the freedom amendment, Lincoln began his new term with the great Second Inaugural Address. Much of his very brief speech was devoted to slavery. After remarking that his audience knew as much about the progress of the war as he did, the President added that at the time of his previous address—

"One-eighth of the whole population were colored slaves, not distributed generally over the Union, but localized in the southern part of it. These slaves constituted a peculiar and powerful interest. All knew that this interest was, somehow, the cause of the war. To strengthen, perpetuate, and extend this interest was the object for which the insurgents would rend the Union, even by war; while the government claimed no right to do more than to restrict the territorial enlargement of it.

"Neither party expected for the war the magnitude or the duration which it has already attained. Neither anticipated that the cause of the conflict might cease with, or even before, the conflict itself should cease. Each looked for an easier triumph, and a result less fundamental and astounding. Both read the same Bible, and pray to the same God; and each invokes His aid against the other. It may seem strange that any men should dare to ask a just God's assistance in wringing their bread from the sweat of other men's faces; but let us judge not, that we be not judged. The prayers of both could not be answered—that of neither has been answered fully.

"The Almighty has his own purposes. 'Woe unto the world because of offenses! For it must needs be that offenses come; but woe to that man by whom the offenses cometh.' If we shall suppose that American slavery is one of those offenses which, in the providence of God, must needs come, but which, having continued through His appointed time, He now wills to remove, and that He gives to both North and South this terrible war, as the woe due to those by whom the offense came, shall we discern therein any departure from those divine attributes which the believers in a living God always ascribe to him?

"Fondly do we hope—fervently do we pray—that this mighty scourge of war may speedily pass away. Yet, if God wills that it continue until all the wealth piled by the bondsman's two hundred and fifty years of unrequited toil shall be sunk, and until every drop of blood drawn with the lash shall be paid by another drawn with the sword, as was said three thousand years ago, so still it must be said, 'The judgments of the Lord are true and righteous altogether.'

"With malice toward none; with charity for all; with firmness in the right, as God gives us to see the right, let us strive on to finish the work we are in; to bind up the nation's wounds; to care for him who shall have borne the battle and for his widow, and his orphan—to do all which may achieve and cherish a just and a lasting peace among ourselves, and with all nations."

Less than a week before Lincoln made his memorable address Congress had made it clear that "malice toward none" and "charity toward all" was not the order of the day on the Hill. Charles Sumner had threatened to filibuster to prevent Senate action on acknowledging the new Unionist government that had been established in Louisiana, and Congress had adjourned without acting in the matter.

This civilian government had been formed, at Lincoln's behest, in the conquered portion of the state. Twelve thousand voters in twenty-eight counties (or parishes, as they are called in Louisiana) had elected a governor and three congressmen. Lincoln had written the new governor, Michael Hahn, to say, "I congratulate you on having fixed your name in history as the first free-state governor of Louisiana. Now you are about to have a convention which, among other things, will probably define the elective franchise. I barely suggest for your private consideration, whether some of the colored people may not be let in—as, for instance, the very intelligent, and especially those who have fought gallantly in our ranks. They would probably help, in some trying time to come, to keep the jewel of liberty within the family of freedom. But this is only a suggestion, not to the public, but to you alone."

A state convention later adopted a constitution which gave the ballot to white males and empowered the state legislature to extend the franchise to Negro soldiers who served in the Union Army and to Negroes who could read and write—the qualifications which Lincoln had suggested to Hahn. During the squabble over the readmission of Louisiana into the Union Lincoln wrote: "A very fair

proportion of the people of Louisiana have inaugurated a
new state government, making an excellent new constitution—better for the poor black man than we have in Illinois."

When Lincoln delivered his Second Inaugural Address
the end of the war was in sight. General William Tecumseh
Sherman had finished his devastation march through
Georgia; General Phil Sheridan had swept the grey riders
from the Shenandoah Valley, which had long been the private preserve of Jackson's Foot Cavalry; Grant had pushed
Lee back through the Wilderness and was about to break
the thin grey line that held the works around Petersburg.
For all practical purposes the Confederacy was reduced to
the Carolinas and part of Virginia. Congress would not
reassemble until next December. Lincoln could move forward with full vigor to lay the foundation for his reconstruction program.

This program was based on his contention that the
southern states had never left the Union, and therefore the
re-establishment of normal relations could be accomplished
within existing law. As in Louisiana, he proposed that
each state would set up a loyal government, with a state
constitution which prohibited slavery, and return representatives to the national Congress. He made recommenda-
tions as to Negro suffrage, but in general he proposed to
deal with the problems of Negro civil rights by attacking
it step by step—in very much the same moderate way as he
had dealt with emancipation. He wanted full civil rights
for Negroes, but felt that the only way this could be accomplished was by a patient course that was divorced from
the passions, malice and fanaticism of the war.

In this he was opposed by the hard core of abolitionists
who wanted immediate, complete, abstract justice for the

Negro even if it meant Negro governments in southern states, established and maintained by northern bayonets. Also, the radical Republicans were far more interested in keeping southern Democrats out of the Congress than they were in the rights of Negroes. To both these groups full Negro suffrage was a "must" requirement for the admission of a southern state.

Lincoln planned to use the months before Congress re-assembled to develop public opinion for his point of view. In this he would be aided by the popular military heroes of the moment. Grant, Sherman and most of the corps commanders agreed with Lincoln—as did, for what it was worth, Lee, Longstreet and Alexander Stephens, the South's vice president.

But fate ordained that Lincoln would speak only once, after the war ended, on the future of the nation and the Negro. It was the evening of April 11, 1865—two days after Lee's surrender at Appomattox. This was a day of cele-bration in Washington, with bands, parades and, after dark, rockets and illuminated buildings. The President had worked all day on the paper which he would deliver from the balcony of the White House that night. Noah Brooks, a Massachusetts newspaper correspondent who was very close to Lincoln, wrote, "There was something terrible in the enthusiasm with which the Chief Executive was re-ceived. Cheers upon cheers, wave after wave of applause rolled up, the President patiently standing quiet until it was all over." Then Lincoln started to read the speech which he held in his right hand, lighting it with a candle held in his left. Brooks reached out from behind a drapery and took the candle from him. Little Tad Lincoln scram-bled around his father's feet picking up the pages as the President dropped each as he finished reading it.

The crowd expected to hear a great victory speech and for a few paragraphs all went well, with references to Grant and his brave men—cheers—the gallant navy—cheers. Then the subject changed and for the remainder of the long speech the crowd fidgeted while the President delivered a carefully reasoned but somewhat heavy and dull exposition of his plan for reconstruction. He reminded his hearers that he had first proposed a plan in his message to Congress of December of 1863. The Cabinet had approved. So had the Congress. Now that Louisiana had formed a government in accordance with that plan, Congress opposed its acceptance. Lincoln defended the Louisiana government's position on Negro suffrage, saying, "It is also unsatisfactory to some that the elective franchise is not given to the colored man. I would myself prefer that it were now conferred on the very intelligent, and on those who serve our cause as soldiers. Still, the question is not whether the Louisiana government, as it stands, is quite all that is desirable. The question is, will it be wiser to take it as it is and help to improve it, or to reject and disperse it?"

In relation to the southern states in general, as well as Louisiana, the President said, "We, in effect, say to the white man: You are worthless or worse; we will neither help you, nor be helped by you. To the blacks we say: This cup of liberty which these, your old masters, held to your lips we will dash from you, and leave you to the chances of gathering the spilled and scattered contents in some vague and undefined when, where, and how. If this course, discouraging and paralyzing both white and black, has any tendency to bring Louisiana into proper practical relations with the Union, I have, so far, been unable to perceive it. If, on the contrary, we recognize and sustain the new government of Louisiana, the converse of all this is made true. We encourage the hearts and nerve the arms of 12,000 to adhere to their work, and argue for it, and proselyte for it, and fight for it, and feed it, and grow it, and ripen it to a complete success.

"The colored man, too, in seeing all united for him, is inspired with vigilance, and energy, and daring, to the same end. Grant that he desires the elective franchise, will he not attain it sooner by saving the already advanced steps toward it than by running backward over them?

"Concede that the new government of Louisiana is only to what it should be as the egg is to the fowl, we shall sooner have the fowl by hatching the egg than by smashing it."

This was Lincoln's last public word on slavery or the future of the freed Negroes. Three days later his plans and hopes for the future would die with him by the action of a crazed, frustrated actor. He did not know, nor did anyone, the contents of a sealed letter which John Wilkes Booth had left with his sister five months before—a letter in which he justified the deed which he planned (at that time the kidnapping rather than the assassination of the President). In it Booth set down the concept of slavery which motivated his scrambled mind.

"People of the North, to hate tyranny, to love liberty and justice, to strike at wrong and oppression, was the teaching of our fathers. The study of our early history will not let me forget it, and may it never.

"This country was formed for the *white,* not for the black man. And, looking upon *African slavery* from the same standpoint held by the noble framers of our Constitution, I, for one, have ever considered *it* one of the greatest blessings (both for themselves and us) that God ever bestowed upon a favored nation. Witness heretofore our wealth and power; witness their elevation and enlightenment above their race elsewhere. I have lived among it most of my life, and have seen *less* harsh treatment from master to man that I have beheld in the North from father to son. Yet, Heaven knows, *no one* would be more willing to do *more* for the negro race than I, could I but see a way to *still better their* condition. But Lincoln's policy is only preparing the way for their total annihilation."

As Lincoln's funeral train slowly chugged toward Illinois one of the thousands of eulogies to the Great Emancipator was delivered by Henry Ward Beecher. While Lincoln lived, Beecher, the abolitionist, had been a constant, nagging critic. Now, more actor than cleric, he used his great powers of oratory in fulsome praise of the departed President—and blamed his assassination on the institution of slavery, describing Booth as a natural outgrowth of the cruel and boisterous passions of the slave system.

"Slavery," thundered Beecher, "wastes its victims, and destroys the masters. . . . It corrupts manhood in its very centre and elements. Communities in which it exists are not to be trusted. They are rotten. . . . The honour that grows up in the midst of slavery is not honour, but a bastard quality." The rebellion, the war, the assassination, all resulted from "that disease of slavery which is a deadly poison to soul and body." Never, said the speaker, would men forget that the slavery institution with its "mischiefs and monsters" had martyred one American President. "Never! while time lasts, while heaven lasts, while hell rocks and groans."

Perhaps the last words on slavery should be said by

Lincoln. He said them many years before his death, during his debates with Stephen Douglas; and, like so much that he said, they were prophetic. "That," said Lincoln, "is the issue that will continue in this country when these poor tongues of Judge Douglas and myself shall be silent. It is the eternal struggle between two principles. The one is the common right of humanity, and the other the divine right of kings. It is the same spirit that says, 'You toil and work and earn bread, and I'll eat it.' No matter in what shape it comes, whether from the mouth of a king who seeks to bestride the people of his own nation and live by the fruit of their labor, or from one race of men as an apology for enslaving another race, it is the same tyrannical principle."

Index